ENDORSEMENTS & REVIEWS

We were both delighted to read such practical and creative ideas on how grandparents can more fully engage in the lives of their grandchildren. This book is not up-in-the-clouds, but down-to-earth where real life takes place. Read and be encouraged! You can make all the difference in the world.

— **Reverend Mark R. Stromberg,** Superintendent of the Northwest Conference of the Evangelical Covenant Church of America and his wife, **Terri Stromberg**

What delightful insights into the grandparent relationship! I believe Carol and Becky tickled every tantalizing emotion possible for grandparents who truly want to be involved in the spiritual lives of their grandchildren.

— **Ginger Craven,** grandmother of eight teenagers

Well-written and engaging, **Faithful Grandparenting** *is a biblical resource packed with creativity and practical applications. Becky and Carol understand our deep desire to connect to our grandchildren and to impact their lives in meaningful and godly ways. Full of shared stories and personal testimony as well as relevant "banners" that highlight key principles and tips, this book ought to be in every grandparent's toolbox as their guide to Christ-centered grandparenting.*

— **Lynda Barger,** M.D. Child and Adolescent Psychiatrist, grandmother of two

Concise and packed full of wisdom and practical ideas, **Faithful Grandparenting** *is a must-read for grandparents who wish to maintain and improve their relationships with both grandchildren and the children's parents. The authors share marvelous ideas regarding communication, discipline, fun activities, traditions, and ways to support spiritual growth. Their suggestions are delightfully useful and are sure to create stronger family bonds in this changing world.*

— ***Laurie Cockerell,*** Conservative Children's Books, Author of *Founders' Fables, Magnificent Sam, The Miracle, The Spirit of Texas,* teacher and social worker, homeschooling mom, Charlie's grandmama

Carol and Becky's hearts for Christ and love for family overflow through the pages of this book. With wise, practical advice, their goal is to equip all of us to be the parents and grandparents God intends us to be. From illustrations of their grandparenting principles to check-the-box ideas, this book should be read time and time again. These are GRAND ideas to connect the generations!

— ***Shug Burg,*** Founder and President of HIM4Her Ministries, radio host, speaker, leader, and evangelist

__Faithful Grandparenting__ is full of practical wisdom and ideas that provide an easy-to-follow roadmap to helping kids and grandkids find their way thoughtfully and intentionally in the world through the families God has given them. Everyone I talk to is looking for practical advice on how to bring the best of themselves into their relationships, and this book will serve many on their journey of extending their influence to the next generation. I'm excited for the way this book will bless grandparents and grandchildren!

— __Thomas Petey Crowder,__ Senior Pastor
Christ Presbyterian Church,
Edina, MN

Having been a grandmother myself for many years, this book reminded me in a fresh and down to earth way, that the things I value most in my life are important enough to pass on to my grandchildren. I was delighted by the creative ways the authors encouraged me to do this in ways I have never imagined. I am challenged to use the examples given in this book to deepen my relationship with each of my unique grandchildren. Thanks for the inspiration!

— __Mary Meyer,__ grandmother of four grandchildren

Mimi is my newest name and role. My husband and I have just stepped into the grandparent phase. We desire to have a strong bond with our grands. We hope to partner with and support our adult children in developing their children's faith. **Faithful Grandparenting** *is filled with wise nuggets and easily applicable ideas for those who want a heart and soul connection with their grands. If you are a grandparent, this book is an invaluable resource, one to which you will refer many times as your grands grow from littles to bigs.*

— **Lori Wildenberg,** speaker, podcaster, licensed parent educator, and author or co-author of 6 parenting books including *The Messy Life of Parenting;* loriwildenberg.com

I highly recommend **Faithful Grandparenting: Practical Ideas for Connecting Generations.**

This book is a must for all grandparents ... whether you are seasoned or just beginning this rich adventure, there are important tools to assist you in sharing your faith with the next generation.

Life today is hectic for most families and having hands-on grandparents who have developed a relationship with their grandchildren from birth can play a key role in each child's life. Becky and Carol have done a marvelous job expressing the joy of grandparenting with lots of practical tips and fun ideas you will want to implement and examples from other grandparents. My husband, Ed, and I consider it a true gift from God to be grandparents of eight amazing grandchildren! This is a wonderful tool for grandparents.

— **Berrie Lounsberry,** founder of The Berry Patch School, grandmother of 8

Loved the book! **Faithful Grandparenting** *is a wonderful guide for grandparents. It not only provides a strong Christian influence, but calls for logical, commonsense grandparenting. I love the way the authors have empowered the reader to highlight key points with the check-off boxes. Being a former athlete and coach, I especially loved the inclusion "Rules of an Athlete." It is "right-on" advice for kids as student athletes!* **Faithful Grandparenting** *is a great contribution to grandparents, present and future!*

— **Dave Appelhof,** grandparent of 12 grandchildren and 2 great grandkids

As the mother of three, I found this book centered on faithful grandparenting to be truly eye-opening. As a survival manual and guidebook, it's filled with tips, not just for grandparents, but for parents, aunts, uncles, and any adults working with children. **Faithful Grandparenting** *is loaded with biblical foundations, tips, fun and creative ideas, and great conversation starters. Thank you, for adding Waters of Wisdom to God's Family Tree.*

— **Barbara Peterson Burwell,** wife, mother, businesswoman, author, philanthropist, Miss USA 1976

As a grandmother to 10 grandchildren, I was greatly inspired by the practical suggestions to make the most of the important role of grandparent. I was given practical suggestions and inspirational stories to guide me. I am praising God for the ways we can make Him known through our love and service to our families as grandparents.

— ***Beverly Coniaris,*** Bible study teacher, grandmother of 10

Faithful Grandparenting: Practical Ideas for Connecting the Generations *is a faithful tribute to grandparenting. Thank you for this wonderful celebration of the importance and rewards of grandparenting. Framed in scripture, the book identifies many attributes and philosophies that contribute to powerful interrelationships. It is a beautiful roadmap full of the "hows" and "whys" on how to better navigate and enjoy the adventures of grandparenting. This book gave my wife and me many thoughts on connecting with our teenage grandchildren. The statements "grandparents are the stabilizing roots of the family tree" and "storytellers of the family history" gave us new vision on connecting with the grandchildren as they mature into adulthood. We have felt that we were "pretty good" grandparents, now we are on the road to become "great" grandparents! Thanks, again, Becky and Carol, for this tribute to the art of grandparenting.*

— ***Ron Hoffman,*** investment management executive,
grandfather of four

This book is a "must-have" resource for every grandparent! You will want to keep this practical and creative book handy as it is filled with ideas for you and your grandchildren. It is also framed within Christ-centered theology that uses scripture to support you in modeling your faith to your grandchildren. There are abundant thoughtful and wise tips for new and not-so-new grandparents. This book will help you be proactive in making effective choices with your grandchildren (and their parents) rather than reacting to issues as they arise. As a grandmother to six grandchildren, I highly recommend **Faithful Grandparenting** *as a grandparent's guide that you will want to have on hand as you navigate the years ahead with your grandchildren.*

— **Beverly Lonsbury,** Ph.D., pastoral care and counseling, grandmother of six

Carol and Becky are both very committed Christians whose education and experience with children and families definitely qualify them to write this meaningful book regarding Christian grandparenting. **Faithful Grandparenting** *is a very comprehensive sharing of concrete relational concepts and activity ideas that will help enrich the relationship between grandparents and their grandchildren. The tie that binds this all together is the consistent reference to Bible verses which support the concepts presented.*

— **Judy Smith,** MA in Supervision and Curriculum in Elementary Education, grandmother of five

Faithful Grandparenting

Faithful Grandparenting

Practical Ideas for Connecting the Generations

They will still bear fruit in old age,
they will stay fresh and green ...
PSALM 92:14

Becky Danielson & Carol Olsen

EQUIP
P R E S S

Faithful Grandparenting

Copyright © 2021 Becky Danielson and Carol Olsen

Library of Congress Cataloging-in-Publication Data

Scripture quotations taken from *The Holy Bible, New International Version, Zondervan Publishing, Grand Rapids, Michigan, Copyright 2011, unless otherwise indicated.*

Cover designer—Elyona Davis
Interior designer—Art Innovations
Editor—Bridgett Harris

Printed in the United States of America.

First Edition: 2021
Faithful Grandparenting / Becky Danielson and Carol Olsen
Paperback ISBN: 978-1-951304-58-4
eBook ISBN: 978-1-951304-59-1

EQUIP
PRESS

DEDICATION

This book is dedicated to Kit Kat, my darling grandmother, who laid a strong foundation of faith, family, and friendship with her grandchildren.

— Becky

This book is dedicated to my eight amazing grandchildren who have widened my world and given me great joy: Lilly, Freja, Ilsa, Olivia, Aidan, Finn, Gabby, and Keenan.

— Carol

Faithful Grandparenting: Practical Ideas for Connecting the Generations *is also dedicated to all the grandparents and grandchildren who contributed ideas, stories, prayers, and strategies for bringing faith and love into GRAND relationships. The willingness to share thoughts, impressions, disappointments, humor, and advice is deeply appreciated. There is great hope for future generations in the love, support, and encouragement of grandparents and seasoned seniors.*

To our Discerning Women, we owe you a debt of gratitude for encouraging us to write this book!

And, most importantly, to the Lord, who has knit each one of our families together.

CONTENTS

Introduction

Grandchildren are amazing! They are darling bundles of joy, your baby's babies, and the continuation of the family legacy, all wrapped into one package. Whether the first or the fifteenth grandchild, each one carries the promise of life and love. The newest additions to the family tree will become the ones entrusted to pass on your family history, traditions, and faith for generations to come.

Grandparents can be a terrific influence on younger generations. There's a tremendous opportunity to speak truth into the lives of grandkids. Unfortunately, many grandparents are finding the task difficult, *really* difficult!

YOU ARE IMPORTANT

Grandparents are truly needed as role models, guides, and confidants for grandchildren. But wait, there's more! We've put together a list of reasons grandchildren need their grandparents. Not every point may fit your situation, but all are valid reasons for grandparenting well.

TOP EIGHT REASONS GRANDCHILDREN *NEED* THEIR FAITH-FILLED GRANDPARENTS

1. Grandparents are stabilizing roots of the family tree.
2. Grandparents exemplify faith in Jesus Christ.

3. Grandparents love unconditionally.

4. Grandparents can often be more flexible with their time than parents.

5. Grandparents are the storytellers of family history.

6. Grandparents have gained wisdom from lifelong experiences.

7. Grandparents are often eager to be part of a grandchild's life.

8. Grandparents can be FUN!

Too often the role of grandparenting is delegated to the grandmother. Grandfathers, you are important, too! Children gain an immeasurable amount of wisdom and positive training from both grandmothers *and* grandfathers. Stepping in to be a role model is vital, especially if children are being raised by a single parent. Children need the support and guidance of strong male and female role models.

Love comes from God. Wisdom comes with age. Service comes from the desire to be the hands and feet of Christ. A grandparent has all three to offer grandchildren. In Psalm 92, we are reminded age has no relevance on the ability to love, lead, and serve. "They will still bear fruit in old age. They will stay fresh and green ..." (Psalm 92:14).

> **Love comes from God. Wisdom comes with age. Service comes from a desire to be the hands and feet of Christ. A grandparent has all three to offer to grandchildren.**

The role of grandparents has changed dramatically from past generations. Today's culture has made extended family relationship building challenging. With the ever-changing landscape of families due to job transitions, living away from extended family, strained relationships, divorce, and single parent homes, the job of grandparenting is challenging. You may be wondering:

- How do grandparents fit into the equation of family life?
- How do grandparents share life lessons and experiences with the next generation?
- How can grandparents effectively influence and support children and grandchildren in a positive and constructive way?

GETTING THE MOST FROM *FAITHFUL GRANDPARENTING*

Grandparenting is exciting, satisfying, and stimulating. Our goal is to give grandparents user-friendly ideas to lead younger generations to a vibrant faith in Jesus Christ and to equip grandparents with ideas to develop strong relational connections. The book is a guide to assist grandmothers and grandfathers in making the most of love, wisdom, and provision for future generations. Each chapter defines a concept related to grandparenting. At the end of each chapter, you'll find "**In Summary: Banners from the Bleachers**" — a synopsis of the key principles and tips to guide and encourage you to intentionally make connections with grandchildren. "*Banners*" is a play on words because it has a double meaning. A banner can be a flag in the bleachers, as if grandparents are cheering on the grandkids. Banners also mark good and guiding principles.

The ideas, information, and suggestions are designed to give grandparents "food for thought" in how to make lasting relationships, build connections, and find enjoyment while sharing faith in Jesus, the family's story, and wisdom with grandchildren. The pages are filled with creative and fun ideas for intentional relationship building. For many grandparents, this book can be used to enhance the grandchild's faith development. For others, the grandparents may be the only connection grandchildren have to learn about Jesus. Each relationship is different and, therefore, no one way fits everyone. Thus, this book has a plethora of ideas and strategies.

You'll find many practical and exciting ideas, thoughts, and suggestions from seasoned grandparents. Each idea or recommendation is preceded by a box (❑) for your convenience. If the idea resonates with you or it's one you wish to remember, check the box for future reference. If you use a colored pen or pencil, the ideas will be easier to find as you flip back through the book. Also, updated resources, new ideas, and the latest in grandparenting is available online at FaithfulGrandparenting.com.

> "This topic is very exciting because I did not have grandmas in my life — one died when I was two and the other was mostly ill and died a bit later and never had time for a relationship or much influence. Couple that with the fact that I grew up in a home where scripture was not studied or discussed by parents or grandparents. As a result, I didn't do well at doing that with my kids since I was spending most of my early 'mom life' learning scripture myself for the first time! So, I have often thought — I have another chance with my grandchildren."
>
> — Katie

In each personal quest to be a *GRAND* grandparent, you will walk alongside two perspectives on grandparenting, one from a seasoned grandma of eight grandchildren (Carol) and one from a granddaughter who was nurtured by an amazing grandma (Becky). We both have studied family education and have worked with families over the years, giving insight and gaining depth into the joys and sorrows of each stage of life. Whether you are new at grandparenting or have been grandparenting for years, *Faithful Grandparenting: Practical Ideas for Connecting the Generations* will support, encourage, and guide you in your role as a GRAND grandparent. Join us!

IDEAS TO APPLY

❏ Check the boxes with a colored pen or pencil for future reference.

❏ Visit *FaithfulGrandparenting.com* for resources, new ideas, and the latest in grandparenting tips and tools.

CHAPTER 1

Embrace Your Role

"Children have a way of being brutally honest. They let you know right away you're Grandma, not Mama," exclaimed Grandma Martha with a chuckle. One of her favorite grand stories happened when she was babysitting her four-year-old granddaughter. The little girl wanted a grilled cheese sandwich, so Martha dutifully started the preparation.

"When I called my granddaughter to the table and set the grilled cheese sandwich in front of her, she burst into tears and told me, 'You made it all wrong Grandma! You don't know how to make a grilled cheese at all!'"

The problem? Grandma Martha had cut the sandwich in half horizontally and the little girl's mother cut it diagonally. Many hugs resolved the problem of the miss-cut sandwich and the real reason for the reaction: missing mom.

Sound familiar?

If you are new at this grandparenting thing, congratulations! Your child has had a child and you have now "graduated" from parent to grandparent. This exciting transition comes with some vital adjustments. An analogy to better understand this shift is with a baseball team.

- With God's help, you selected the co-owner (your spouse) and, over time, "the team" (child/children) began to form via birth, adoption, or marriage. Your responsibilities within the team expanded to coach, manager, and referee. On the field, you were directing, teaching, disciplining, and making final calls.
- However, as the children matured, other "coaches" arrived, assuming many of the duties. You were still involved in the day-to-day business management of the team but were no longer on the field full-time. From the dugout, you were critiquing plays, giving advice, mending injuries, and encouraging team members.
- Eventually, the team expands with your children's friends and future spouse. New team members, new plays, changing rules, and differing assumptions are all part of your changing role.
- Finally, when your kids start their own family (a brand-new team), there are adjustments. Often at this point, many grandparents take on the role of a cheerleader in the stands. This is an essential role because cheering a child to a purposeful and faithful life is just as important as being the immediate coach. But more than likely, you may be called back to the playing field to fulfill other roles.

Once a parent, you're always a parent, but the relationship with a grandchild is different from parenting your own child. It can be a hard adjustment going through the stages listed above, from being in control to becoming a cheerleader. But there's beauty in the transition. The way you react to "plays" can create tension or confidence in the new team. It's a choice you make, to support and encourage or dislike and discourage. Embrace your role as grandparent, not parent.

Each family is different. Some parents are very casual about the grandparent's involvement with their child, but some are much more guarded.

> Be the family member that loves unconditionally, forgives readily, and encourages often.

When watching from the bleachers, expect everyone on the team to do his or her best. This includes the grandparent in the stands! Be the family member that loves unconditionally, forgives readily, and encourages often.

GRANDPARENT INVENTORY

Take time to examine your view of grandparenting by looking at your goals and preferences. Here are questions that will help you determine how you can make connections and build a strong relationship with your grandchildren.

- What role do you hope to play in your grandchild's life?
- What are your biggest concerns about being a grandparent?
- Do busyness and chaos bother you?
- Do you prefer one-on-one or group gatherings?
- What time of day are you at your best: morning, afternoon, evening?
- How will you pray for and share your faith with your grandchild?

- What makes you unique?
- What interests, hobbies, and abilities can you share with your grandchild?
- What adventures would you like to share with your grandchild?

YOUR NEW TITLE

Great-grandmother Judy shared how much she wanted to be a grandmother. In fact, when she was first married, she told her husband she couldn't wait to be a grandmother. Her own grandmother was delightful. Judy's husband, Jim, just smiled and said, "Remember, first you need to be a mother. Have patience."

When a grandchild arrives, you get the new and exciting title of GRANDPARENT. It's a great big title! What do you want to be called: Papa, Grandpa, Nana, Mimi, Sugar, GG, Bumpa, Duke? Think ahead to help eliminate an unwanted nickname. Maybe you have a favorite nickname, or your family has a tradition of a pet name that is used for grandparents. Google a list of other options. Talk to your kids and their spouses to get their input, too. Grandma Nancy chose "Sugar." Now that's a sweet name!

Great-grandfather Chuck became frustrated trying to determine what his great grandchildren would call him. His son was their grandfather and had the same first name, but he did not want to be called the same name, Grandpa Chuck. He found the perfect solution using his full name, Chuck Irvine. He admitted it sounded rather strange coming from a little one, but he'll be remembered in a unique way.

You may end up with two names, or even a different name for each family if you have multiple families with grandchildren. One grandparent is Nana to one family and Grandma Sally to another. With a chuckle, she admits sometimes she forgets who she is! If you're new to grandparenting, the other set of grandparents may already have a nickname with older grandkids. Two Nanas and two Papas can be fine, just work it out with other family members.

What makes you unique? Are you a cookie baker, big hugger, sports fan, or jokester? What kind of games do you like to play? This will change as the children grow, but it's fun to think about how you'll impact your grandchildren with your interests and hobbies.

What special trips would you like to take with grandchildren? These can be overnight, daytrips to a local museum, or even extensive travel. Plan ahead and talk with your children and their spouses regarding any special trips you'd like to take with extended family members or just the grandchildren.

ENCOURAGE AND SUPPORT

New parents need love and encouragement, not condemnation and criticism. Every child is different. New parents are often unsure concerning this great responsibility of raising a child. Anything you can do to support the new family will be appreciated. How you phrase a comment can make all the difference. You probably remember how you responded to unsolicited advice when you were a new mom or dad. New parents are learning how to navigate marriage and family life. Different ideas and suggestions from culture, books,

> New parents need love and encouragement, not condemnation and criticism.

the internet, doctors, and other educators are flooding the parenting field. Encourage common sense and godly parenting.

Fairness, equality, and consistency are needed with all children, in-laws, and grandchildren. You may relate more easily with one child than another. At all costs, avoid favoritism. Comparison kills relationships. Playing favorites creates friction. Unfortunately, competition between families is part of human nature. Work to keep it at a minimum.

Some grandchildren will need more support from you. Some will be more appreciative of the things you do. Some will be more interested in spending time with you. No matter what, try to be fair. This can be especially true when grandparenting a combination of biological, step-, and adopted grandchildren. Grandparents can be either a uniting force or a dividing force in what is often a delicate family unit. You may be one of multiple grandparents. Find a way to be fair to all. Keep in mind, gossiping and talking about parents (your adult child/spouse) or taking sides against parents is a recipe for disaster for you, the parents, and your grandchildren.

Another way to unite the family is to be present when your child's family is going through hard times with challenges that likely affect your grandchildren. For example, call your grandchild frequently, allowing the child to share events from the day at school. Children need to have someone to talk to about their activities. You can be that listening ear.

Empower your grandchildren in all aspects of life. Being "good" to a grandchild doesn't mean bribing or enabling him or her with money, clothing, or food — or accepting poor behavior. Grandparents are not called to be vending machines! Balance is needed. Help grandchildren make healthy choices. Shower them with hugs and kisses (and sometimes treats and special gifts) but avoid spoiling them too much. Making excuses for poor behavior enables grandchildren and doesn't allow for personal responsibility. Enabling can be a trap. Take heed, you don't need to be a Rockefeller to spoil a child. Support and encouragement need to be unifying, fair, and consistent.

FUN TIME TOGETHER

F.U.N. can be synonymous with G.R.A.N.D.P.A.R.E.N.T. in many ways. After years of doing the hard work of parenting, we can enjoy our child's kids. But leaving Mom and Dad out of the plan is not a good idea. Although the phrase, "What happens at Grandma and Grandpa's stays at Grandma and Grandpa's," is trendy, we recommend that honesty and transparency are better in the long run.

> F.U.N. can be synonymous with G.R.A.N.D.P.A.R.E.N.T. in many ways.

Grandma Crag had great advice: "Dance with your grandkids!" Keep in contact with each one. Show that you have a sense of humor. Make your time together fun even if it is doing something simple like playing games or singing songs. After she passed away, her grandkids produced a video of dancing and singing in honor of their special little grandmother and played it at many family gatherings.

IDEAS TO APPLY

☐ Play Peek-A-Boo with little ones, laughing to encourage giggles. Learn songs, fingerplays, and nursery rhymes with actions to teach and sing with the grandchildren.

❑ At your home, provide a "Busy Box" for small grandchildren. Give them access to a box or a drawer filled with special activities such as toys, puzzles, crayons, books, cars ... whatever they like. Needless to say, they will make a beeline for the box as soon as they arrive, hopefully after a big hug, of course. Change the items as the children mature.

❑ Build a tent fort with blankets and pillows. Grandchildren love cozy hiding places.

❑ Play board games or cards. Start with something simple like the board game Candy Land.® Work up to Monopoly® or other favorites. Grandpa Gene was very proud of his six-year-old grandson when, at a museum, the curator asked if anyone knew the name of the board game in a 1940 display. The grandson raised his hand and said, "Parcheesi! My grandfather and I play it all the time!" You can go online and get instructions for old card games you remember from childhood.

❑ Sleepovers are great fun for the grandchildren, especially when cousins can be together. However, they can be very exhausting for grandparents. A great idea is to have one or two movies available for the evening. Preview the movie, even if the movie was recommended by a friend, since standards and opinions can vary. Find ones that demonstrate Christian principles and moral values. Include fun foods and beverages, too! Better yet, include the grandkids in the planning and preparation.

❑ One grandmother tied a treat or prize to the end of a big ball of yarn. She strung several balls of yarn throughout the house, over and under the furniture, like a spider's web. When the grandkids came to her house, they each received a ball with their name on it and had to untangle the web to find their gift.

❑ A great activity for all ages is a whiteboard, washable markers, and a dry eraser. With these supplies, any age child can draw pictures or play games without much of a mess. You may want to have two or three small whiteboards available if you have several grandchildren visiting at once.

❑ Flashlights are fun in a dark room. Teach your grandchildren to make finger designs and characters for shadow stories.

❑ Plan a scavenger hunt. If appropriate, let the grandchildren have free run of the neighborhood. (You may want to forewarn the neighbors.) If going to the neighbors or through the neighborhood is not appropriate, you can create a scavenger hunt in your house or apartment. Write clues that send the child from place to place in search of the final treasure.

❑ Grandpa H. created an Escape Room, challenging his grandchildren to solve an assortment of problems and tasks with clues.

❑ Allow for silly fun! Gabby loves to dance with her grandma for funny social media posts. Give dance instructions for the Lindy. Learn some of your grandkids latest dance moves. But grandparent beware the new moves may be a bit more strenuous!

❑ Gram has her eyes peeled each spring for squirt guns and water toys for the kids to use at the lake for outdoor fun. The good-natured water fights have become a tradition for the whole family.

❑ Grandma Ginny always has a game in her purse, usually the Left Center Right™ game. When waiting at a restaurant or for an appointment with her grandchildren, "Grandma's Purse" is a magic method to keep them occupied and entertained.

❑ Make visits fun with treats! Grandma Fran always came to visit with a couple of wrapped Oreo cookies in her pocket. Grandpa Sam always had bubble gum in his pocket and was soon dubbed "Grandpa Bubble Gum." Find the sweet spot (sometimes, literally) with your grandchildren!

❑ Make your home a place the grandkids want to visit. With kid artwork and family photos decorating the home, children will feel appreciated and welcomed.

❑ Pinterest (Pinterest.com) is a terrific social media platform in which to find appropriate ideas. Start your own boards to save the ideas, activities, and recipes you want to try with your grandkids.

IN SUMMARY: BANNERS FROM THE BLEACHERS

- Examine your grandparenting goals and preferences.
- Embrace the transition from parenting to grandparenting.
- Avoid favoritism.
- Grandparents can be a lot of FUN!

CHAPTER 2

Find Ways to Relate

All relationships are different. Sometimes, we naturally click with family members and fall into an easy, relaxed bond. Sometimes, it's the opposite with strained, uncomfortable, or downright tense interactions. Getting along with friends can be easy, but relatives may require more grace. Getting along is the godly choice for the sake of the whole family.

It's the same way with grandchildren. As kids mature, interests, as well as time with extended family, change. Make the most of time spent and connections built with your grandchildren.

QUANTITY TIME *AND* QUALITY TIME

The quality of a relationship with grandchildren is often directly related to the quantity of time spent together. The more time we spend with the ones we love, the more opportunities we have to develop connections. The more connections we make, the stronger the relationship. Do not be discouraged if you live far away. There are creative and intentional ways to connect and build good relationships.

There are both benefits and detriments to living near (or far from) grandchildren. You are a fortunate grandparent if your grandchildren live close and you can spend time with them. You can see them more often. However, because of activities and busy schedules, sometimes it's difficult to establish designated, quality time together. Keep trying!

On the flip side, you are also fortunate if your grandchildren live far away because you can plan to visit for exclusive periods of time. This can provide dedicated times of togetherness by participating in their everyday lives. Both "near and far" have advantages and disadvantages.

> Little Maddie was excited because her grandparents were coming for a visit. She told her friend, "Grandma and Grandpa are great. They live at the airport. Isn't that cool? They have lots of friends there! When we want them to visit, we go get them at the airport, and when they get tired of being with us, we take them back to the airport and drop them off."

If you have several children and their families living close to you, you may run into a different frustration: accommodating everyone and experiencing sheer exhaustion. Try to be fair but know that each situation will require flexibility because of chaotic family calendars. A helpful tip is to be flexible with your calendar. Family schedules consist of the needs, requests, and activities of your adult children and grandchildren. For years, your immediate family lived according to your family schedule, but now, as a grandparent, you'll need to adjust to the fluctuating plans of the young family. Be flexible and accommodating. Make a plan knowing you can change it if necessary. Scheduling problems come with the territory; kids get sick, plans change. Even the weather can be a factor.

Be flexible and accommodating.

Look for special opportunities for spending extra time with your grandchildren. For example, young grandchildren often need a babysitter.

Lending a helping hand with the care of grandchildren is a chance to connect on a more personal level than just holidays and special occasions. Take advantage of this time. Parents will appreciate your assistance for an evening out or even a vacation for just the two of them. An added benefit is giving your children, the parents, time to devote to their marriage relationship. Raising kids is still a full-time job. A stronger marriage creates a more cohesive family unit.

If babysitting is not your thing, you can still be of great help to the parents. Grandma Sarah was not much for babysitting or projects, but she wanted to connect with her grandchild and be helpful to her daughter-in-law. She offered to do the driving to preschool on a regular basis. This turned out to be greatly helpful, especially when her second grandchild arrived. Sarah's daughter-in-law could stay home with the new baby and the preschooler kept up the same routine with grandma.

The bottom line is to be available to the best of your ability. Take advantage of requests for rides to an activity, shopping with older kids, or assisting with childcare because it will provide a time to be together. Connect when you can.

Of course, health issues of either grandparent can take precedence over availability. You may not always be able to be involved. But don't worry, *Faithful Grandparenting: Practical Ideas for Connecting the Generations* will also give you other less physical ways to stay connected.

IDEAS TO APPLY

☐ Offer to do the driving or carpooling for preschool, classes, or other activities. In the car, keep the radio off and listen. Share your own stories. Encourage conversations. You can also run errands, or even make meals.

☐ Give parents time off to "date" and strengthen their marriage by offering to watch the grandchildren.

☐ Offer to be a homework or special project helper.

Families need to be intentional in connecting with one another to build lasting relationships. To best meet the needs of the family, one should plan ahead. Why? Grandkids will be little forever, right? Wrong! Grandkids seem to grow even faster than your own children did. In a blink of an eye, they will go from toddler to young adult. Plant the seed of connection early and watch it grow into a rewarding relationship with each grandchild. Start where you are now, make the move, and intentionally connect with your grandchildren.

INTERACTING WELL

Kids ask the most amusing questions:

"Grandma Ruth, do those cracks in your face hurt?"

"Nana, why don't you have any little kids? I think you should get some little kids of your own!"

Children's questions and literal view of the world are often refreshing. Give grandchildren the present of your presence as a confidant and sounding board. Use good listening skills such as eye contact and repeating back what the child states for clarification. Respond honestly and respectfully.

> A youngster asked his grandfather, "Did God make you?" Grandpa smiled and answered, "Yes, and he also made you." With that the little boy looked puzzled and slowly replied, "He is doing a much better job now."

Be worthy of your grandchild's trust. Always leave the door open for communication on any topic. Unless the conversation crosses into an illegal or immoral issue, be still and actively listen. If the issue is something you feel needs to be discussed with your adult child and his/her spouse, encourage your grandchild to speak to the parents first, and give the grandchild the opportunity to do so. Take action if the parent or grandchild could be harmed if delayed. When necessary, seek help from a pastor, psychologist, the police, or an attorney. Aim for straight thinking and not just emotions. The health and safety of the grandchild are always paramount.

> **Be worthy of your grandchild's trust.**

Be aware of the soapbox! The fine line between listening and sharing is hard to identify. If the grandkids walk away from your conversation prematurely, chances are your "advice" has gone too far. This applies to sharing opinions, too.

T.M.I. (Too Much Information) can be a problem for those who have experienced more of life's challenges or just feel the need to give unsolicited advice. Share opinions when appropriate. Your children and grandchildren can be easily hurt by words and advice. Even if the intention is good, the words can sting.

This goes both ways in families. Our kids' words can be equally hurtful. If at all possible, avoid allowing situations to fester. Be willing to forgive and forget minor offenses. When that's not possible, be upfront in voicing concerns and feelings, showing wisdom and love. Use *"I" statements* to clarify how you feel and what you need, as opposed to *"you" statements* that sound like shame and blame. Avoid use of superlatives like "always" and "never." Try to keep the conversation from becoming heated. Each has one's own take on situations and each has unique emotional responses. Mend fences when at all possible. Winning an argument but losing the relationship is never a good outcome.

Forgiveness is healing to all parties. "Bear with each other and forgive one another if any of you has a grievance against someone. Forgive as the Lord forgave you" (Colossians 3:13). If you've been hurt, forgive and move on. Continuing to hold grudges and expecting the worst from others will make for uncomfortable relationships and stressful family gatherings.

> Conversations create connections. Connections build relationships.

Sharing life events and day-to-day experiences with loved ones is the secret to linking the generations in a healthy and happy manner. Sharing binds family members together. Conversations create connections. Connections build relationships. Finding opportunities is the key. Be purposeful in connecting with the next generation(s).

My grandmother was the best listener! She rarely interrupted me, allowed me to finish my tales, and asked specific questions. I always felt loved and understood. She was trustworthy, too, keeping confidences.

—Becky

How do you challenge your grandkids to *think?* One way is to ask questions regarding their viewpoints. Find out what they believe *and why.* It's not imperative to agree with them, but grandparents do need to pay attention. We need to learn from each other, even from our grandchildren. And children enjoy teaching the adults in their lives. You'll learn games, words, and lots of new technology tips!

Young people today have been educated to think and process differently than their "senior generation" grandparents. Nowadays, kids are taught critical thinking skills that seemingly put an emphasis on the criticizing of standards. Approaching situations with emotions rather than empirical truth has become the norm. In conversations, challenge your grandchildren to stretch their appreciation of diversity, not only for skin color and gender, but for thoughts and opinions, too. Just because one does not like or agree with an opinion does not make it wrong. Grandparents who learn to discuss various subjects without any hostility for varying opinions build relationships. After talking to many grandparents who find it difficult to discuss anything other than the weather, consider the following:

- Which is more important, your opinion or your relationship with your grandchild?
- What are your reasons for your thoughts/beliefs on difficult topics? Write your thoughts down, organized in short sound bites rather than long, rhetorical monologues.
- Are you modeling positive thinking? This does not mean you need to hide or forget your passion and ideas. Just communicate clearly and succinctly, explaining your point of view.

IDEAS TO APPLY

❑ Set a goal: At least one contact, with each grandchild, each month. Some of you will laugh because you have constant contacts, but for some with far away or estranged grandchildren, it can be a difficult goal. You can't control their reaction, but you can reach out.

❑ Make use of cellphones to send daily or weekly messages including positive moral words to live by, funny ideas, jokes, or quotes to keep a connection open. Feedback is fun! Many grandchildren enjoy getting messages.

❑ Stay in touch as you travel by sending postcards to your grandchildren. Before you leave, give each child a metal ring that easily opens and shuts. While traveling, buy post cards, punch a hole in the corner, add a note, and send the cards with a colorful stamp. Your grandkids can put the cards on the ring as a special keepsake. If they are older, encourage them to find your location(s) on a map for a lesson in geography.

❑ Ask your grandchildren what books they are reading for school or pleasure. Then, read that same book. Start a conversation about the characters and overall message. You can also ask what they are studying in history and add to their learning through your discussions. Who knows? You may be able to give firsthand knowledge of the historical event!

❑ Connecting a large family can be done by sending out a newsletter once a month containing family updates. This is especially valuable for families that are scattered around the country or the world. "The Family Times" newsletter can be mailed, emailed, or messaged.

WORDS OF WISDOM

Sharing wisdom from a life well-lived with grandchildren of any age is truly a gift and provides positive direction for children and builds strong relationships. Grandpa Tom found a way to do just that by writing down his thoughts and titled it, "*Some Rules for a Young Athlete*." Grandpa Tom was an athlete when he attended the University of Minne-

> Share wisdom from a life well-lived.

sota. He loved participating in sports and coaching young people. He and his wife, Karen, now have many grandchildren who excel in athletics. He agreed to share his insightful thoughts.

SOME RULES FOR A YOUNG ATHLETE

Rule 1: Don't quit.

When you get knocked down (i.e., lose, make a bad play, miss a shot, fumble a ball ...), get right back up. A winner never quits, and a quitter never wins.

Rule 2: Take care of your body.

Get proper sleep. Work hard at improving strength, quickness, and agility (don't just be content with what you are born with). Avoid drugs, tobacco, alcohol, and other things harmful to your body.

Rule 3: Outwork the opposition.

Commit yourself to outworking your opponent every day. Remember, this includes classmates and teammates, as well as people on the other team.

Rule 4: Constantly improve.

Commit yourself to trying to improve every day. If you are not improving every day, you are not staying the same but are actually going backward (i.e., falling behind) because one (or more) of your opponents is improving.

Rule 5: Know the difference between ability and hard work.

The most successful athletes are not typically born with the greatest ability; rather, they make the most out of the ability they have. The same is true for people in virtually every sector of life (i.e., students, employees, business, politicians, etc.). If you are willing to work hard enough, you can achieve great things.

Rule 6: Be humble.

It's normal human nature to appreciate recognition for a job well done (i.e., good play, victory, test score, or award). A true champion does not talk about his or her accomplishments or otherwise attempt to call attention to himself/herself (e.g., jumping up and down, thumping his chest after making a tackle) but instead, lets actions or performances do the talking. If asked, he/she will respond by speaking about the team's performance rather than his/her own performance.

Rule 7: Consider it a privilege.

When you are representing your school or other organization as a member of a team, consider it a privilege rather than an obligation. (Nothing bothers me more than hearing a young athlete complain about having to go to a practice. Only a relatively few have the opportunity!) If you are going, you are fortunate.

Rule 8: Be successful.

If you outwork your opponent (i.e., the person you are competing against for a position on the team, in a class, for a job, etc.) and, in the process, perform to the maximum extent of your ability, you *will have succeeded* regardless of the score.

Rule 9: Make sacrifices.

To be the best, you have to be willing to sacrifice more. You may have to pass up a party or forego staying up late or even going out with friends when you have to get in a workout, get necessary sleep, prepare for a contest or game, study your assignments, etc.

Rule 10. Operate with integrity.

At all times and in all things, operate with integrity. Tell the truth. Play by the rules. Do not cheat. Do not take shortcuts. If your coach says, "Do 10 pushups," do 20. If he says, "Run a 20-yard wind sprint," run 25 yards, and run as fast as you can even though others may slow down before finishing. When you make a mistake, admit it and don't make excuses.

Rule 11: Follow the "Cardinal Rule."

Learn from defeat, but never accept it. Tomorrow is another day and another opportunity.[1]

Another grandfather, who had served in the Navy, told his grandchildren if they wanted to save the world, they needed to make their beds. This lesson came from U.S. Navy Admiral William H. McRaven's book, *Make Your Bed*. To the grandfather, it was an encouragement to his grandkids to start the day accomplishing something and paying attention to little things. No matter what happens, they will always have a nice bed to welcome them at the end the day.

---

1   Tom Moe, *"Some Rules for a Young Athlete"* Used with permission of the author.

Grandma Janet wanted to share her gems of wisdom for a successful, productive, and moral life with her grandchildren. She put together "Grandma's Top Ten List for a Happy Life."

1. Appreciate marriage and family, the cornerstone of society.
2. Understand the far-reaching consequences in choosing a spouse.
3. Value motherhood and fatherhood.
4. Appreciate the human body created by God, male and female.
5. Be thankful for the liberty and opportunity provided by our country.
6. Educate yourself in history.
7. Recognize unhealthy habits as compared to healthy behaviors.
8. Deal with anxiety and disappointment in a healthy manner.
9. Discern messages expressed in media and entertainment.
10. Recognize the difference between free enterprise and socialism.

Time is precious to young people and usually more abundant for seniors. Grandma Ruth was accommodating to her granddaughter's schedule, making it much easier for her to visit. She always told her granddaughter she would be waiting and not to hurry. It's a great lesson in kindness, patience, and appreciation.

IDEAS TO APPLY

❑ Share your favorite books and authors with your grandchildren. Give books as gifts with a personal note as to why you chose that particular title for your grandchild.

❑ Write down your insights, thoughts, and words of advice and encouragement. Give a copy to each of your grandchildren. For example, Grandpa B. loved quotes and used them to share his philosophy and to train his children, then grandchildren, and now great-grandchildren. The quotes have lived on long after he went to be with the Lord. Here are some of "Grandpa B's Tips for Life":

1. "How do you know you can't if you haven't tried?"
2. "The harder you work, the luckier you will be."
3. "The easiest person to fool is yourself."
4. "The time is always right to do what is right."
5. "Once started, half done."
6. "Patience is a virtue."
7. "You know what you know but you don't know what you don't know."

❑ Grandma Edith started a tradition to save the front page of the newspaper depicting national and world events. Now, her young great grandchildren are interested in such events. She saved newspapers of World War II, the John F. Kennedy assassination, and other historical events. Although so much is available online, how special to have something unique like a newspaper from the actual time period. The "original documents" are a hit for school projects!

IN SUMMARY: BANNERS FROM THE BLEACHERS

- Be flexible with your calendar to be available when needed.
- Share your wisdom.
- A trustworthy grandparent values the relationship more than winning arguments.
- Ask questions to encourage thinking skills.

CHAPTER 3

GRAND Ideas

Cicely had spent a long weekend at grandma and grandpa's house. When her mom and dad arrived to take her home there was a happy reunion with hugs and kisses. As Cicely was slipping into her jacket, she asked her mom, "I wish Grandma June and Grandpa Frank lived next door to our house because they do so many fun things. Do you know we even built a snowman in the bathtub?"

Let's get down to business! How do you connect? You can do really fun things with the grandchildren and then have the option to send them home. This chapter lists ideas and suggestions for children of all ages: *Littles, Middles, and Bigs.* The ideas are sorted by age group, but you know your grandchildren best. Feel free to use any idea to connect with your own grandchildren if you think it's "up their alley."

THE LITTLES

Unless you have a large extended family with children of many ages or work with young children, chances are you haven't been around little ones since your kids were small. These little bundles of joy are amazing. They can sometimes be intimidating, but you can intentionally connect and grow a meaningful relationship at an early age.

❑ As grandbabies grow up, consider safety factors. Childproofing your home may be necessary. Baby gates, outlet plugs, cabinet locks, and other safety devices will make grandma and grandpa's home a safe place for young grandchildren to visit.

❑ If possible, purchase a car seat, highchair, sippy cups, bottles, diapers, and baby spoons to keep at your home. Sometimes, parents can forget these items. It's convenient to have them at your home. Work with the parents (your son/daughter and their spouse) to determine what type of equipment and supplies they prefer and what works best for their family.

❑ Create a "Dress-Up Box" with previously worn prom dresses, costumes like grass skirts, high heels, old jewelry, chaps, a coonskin cap, old letter jackets, etc. Use what you have in your closet or look for items at garage and tag sales. Don't be shy! Dress up with the grandkids!

❑ Grandma Terri created a "Treasure Box" filled with special items, mostly from nature. She used an old cigar box and put in all the special items she found during her early morning walks. The grandkids loved seeing empty eggshells from a robin's nest, Lake Superior rocks, pressed leaves, and other treasures. The kids were always eager to discover Grandma Terri's new additions to the box.

❑ Select a book, maybe one from your youth, and read it to your grandchild. For extra help making the selection, talk to the local children's librarian or a member of the children's ministry staff at your church.

❑ Build an art gallery in your home. Purchase an 8x10 picture frame for each grandchild, put their name on it, and hang it on a special grandchildren's wall that you designate within your home. When your grandchild gives you a gift of special artwork, place each piece of art in the correct frame for each grandchild artist. When it becomes too thick with items, make a folder for each child and tuck the art away in a memory box or make an electronic file with photos of curated art.

❑ Have a few tub toys on hand for bath time and sleepovers. Have extra toothbrushes, too. Buy a little kit and put the child's name on it. Fill it with toothpaste, soap, a comb, and a toothbrush. Little things can feel so special to a child.

❑ Host a tea party. Bring out the china, sugar cubes, and finger sandwiches to entertain in an old-fashioned, high-society way.

❑ Grandma Kim always has a can or two of shaving cream, food coloring, a vinyl tablecloth, and a jellyroll pan handy. Her grandkids love the messiness and squishiness! The clean-up is easy, and the storage is minimal.

❑ Sticker books are a neat and creative way to provide art projects for little children.

❑ Have additional pieces of construction paper available for grandchildren to create greeting cards.

❑ Fill the bathtub or a large container with snow placed on a vinyl sheet or thick towel. Assemble items like a carrot, scarf, buttons, etc., and build a snowman together in the tub.

❑ Matching games are motivational and educational for little ones. Store-bought games are not necessary. Have your grandchild help with the laundry by matching socks.

❑ Fold a paper towel to fit snuggly in a Zip-Loc™ bag. Moisten the paper towel. Help your grandchild arrange bean seeds on the towel. Carefully squeeze air from the bag and seal. Hang the bag in a sunlit window and observe the seeds as they germinate. Turn the bags each week to see how God has designed seedlings to always grow in the proper direction. The roots always go down and the stems always go up. Transplant the seedlings to a garden area or pot.

THE MIDDLES

❑ Create a Refrigerator Gallery. Grandma Ginny attaches each child's school picture (2" x 3") to a small magnetic sheet she purchased at the craft store. Each year, she places the new school photo on her refrigerator to add to the collection. By the time the grandchildren graduate from high school, she can view all their growing up years at once.

❑ Paint craft store birdhouses. Have the grandchildren sign and date each treasure and display them on your porch.

❑ Abuelo Brian (Spanish for Grandpa Brian) bought penny collector books for his grandsons. He found a bag of old coins around the house and then also purchased a bag of coins at a coin shop. The grandsons have fun sorting the coins and even learning about history. Next, he may have to move up to nickels, dimes, and quarters.

❑ Send a little gift once a month to a grandchild far away. The tiny treasure does not have to cost much: a stamp, cartoon, pack of gum, personal note, or photograph of the family.

❑ Remember that "Dress-Up Box"? Now it can provide great costumes for school vintage parties. One beautiful blue prom dress was worn for a middle school 1980s party. Old letter jackets are always a hit.

❑ Message grandchildren a Bible verse every Sunday to remind them of the Lord's Day and provide boost of encouragement for the week ahead. (Great for any age!)

❑ Make sachets with the grandkids. Pick flowers or herbs. Dry the plants by hanging them upside down in a cool, dry place. Crumble the dried plants, add a drop of perfume or essential oil, and fold into a square of cotton or gauze. Tie with a ribbon.

❑ In a milkweed patch, capture a caterpillar. Make a home for the insect in a covered, large glass or plastic container with air vents. Add branches and additional milkweed for food. Observe the caterpillar's metamorphosis to a chrysalis and then, a butterfly. One grandmother told us of the joy she shared with her grandkids in watching the butterfly emerge from the chrysalis and the grandchildren setting the butterfly free outside.

❑ Provide plastic pots, potting soil, and seeds for the grandchildren to grow flowers or vegetables. Help the grandchildren transplant the seedlings into a garden and harvest the produce as it grows. Children get a kick out of specialized gardens too. For example, basil, rosemary, and cherry tomatoes make a pizza garden.

THE BIGS

Before you know it, that sweet little grandbaby is now a young adult, full of abilities and opportunities. You, as a grandparent, are still important because you are modeling the wisdom and grace that comes with a long life. This is the time when the relationships you built in the early years become a gift. And if you haven't built a strong relationship in the early years, it's never too late to start connecting individually with your grandchild.

❑ Gram sent a funny card every week to her four college grandsons and included cash for a treat. It was a blessing for Austin, Ryan, Eric, and David.

❑ College students like to be remembered with some kind of treat right around finals week or really, anytime! Let the college-age grandchildren know you are praying for them too. For example, one grandma fills the college grandkids in on the family happenings and includes a treat with the letter.

❑ Grandchildren living away from home, either in college or working, enjoy receiving notes and gifts from grandpa and grandma. Since postage for packages can be expensive, Grandmother Mary sends beef jerky, which is lightweight and easy to mail. Candy shops are happy to send an individualized gift box to make a college-age grandchild's day brighter. Online shopping provides a way to send a variety of unique surprises. With the advent of email, texting, and social media, actual mail is almost a lost art, so a note or parcel in the mailbox brings a smile.

☐ A great gift idea for students living away from home is to put together an "Advent Box" filled with various small items numbered 1-24. Include Bible verses to keep "the Reason for the season" the focus of the package.

☐ Provide a letter to each grandchild as they graduate from high school or college/trade school explaining how proud you are of them and what a great blessing they are to the family. Include a prayer for God's provision for the grandchild's future.

☐ Let your older grandchildren select a gift from special family treasures you have around your home. Many such gifts are tucked away but make great keepsake gifts. Tell the story behind the item and how it connects to the family. A grandmother shared how her daughter wanted a written history on specific family heirlooms.

☐ There is a window of time for giving family treasures to your kids and grandkids. When grandkids are moving into the world and setting up their own space, they can actually use and appreciate household items and treasures. Purchase or find identical sized boxes for each grandchild. Go through your house and place practical items and heirlooms into each box with approximately the same value per box and then seal it. Allow the grandchild to choose a sealed box at the time of marriage or at age 25. Do this freely and graciously, and keep in mind, once the items are given, they belong to the grandchild and can be kept, donated, or tossed as the grandchild wishes.

☐ Plan a "grand" date. Take your school-age grandchild out for hot chocolate or a smoothie. Encourage discussing a variety of subjects. Ask questions and be a good listener.

Your young adult grandchildren need you, too! This is an exceptionally important time for a grandparent to connect and appreciate who the young person has become as an adult. It's a time of change and often, eye-opening for the older grandchild. Knowing grandma and grandpa care enough to connect provides a layer of security for the grandchild, as well as a connection to the extended family. It's a privilege and pleasure to have a meal and conversation with an adult grandchild. There can be such satisfaction in the mature relationship between grandparent and grandchild.

After living in a college dorm, then a sorority house, and now an apartment, a granddaughter was learning a lot about living on her own. During a conversation with her grandmother, Lilly exclaimed, "Grandma! Do you know how much toilet paper costs?!?"

IN SUMMARY: BANNERS FROM THE BLEACHERS
- Find individual and specific ways to connect with your grandchild.
- Every connection is unique. Make your own personal roadmap.
- There's an opportunity to connect with all ages.

CHAPTER 4

Encourage Faith, Gratitude, and Honesty

The grandchildren were visiting from out of town on Sunday, so grandma and grandpa took the whole family to church. When the pastor asked the children to come up to the front for the Children's Message, Sammy did not want to go. After much encouragement, he joined the other children. The pastor, being a kindly sort, asked Sammy, "What is furry, has a big tail, and climbs trees?" Sammy thought for a moment and in sheer desperation said, "It sounds like a squirrel, but I know it must be Jesus."

MAKE A GRAND DIFFERENCE

With the beautiful gift of grandparenting comes the responsibility of encouraging children to accept Jesus and follow his teachings. "Start children off on the way they should go, and even when they are old they will not turn from it" (Proverbs 22:6). Demonstrate behavior that is honoring to Christ. Some grandchildren will have many opportunities to be discipled by followers of Jesus. Others may have just you, but God provides, and you will be enough!

Every grandchild will have difficulties and heartbreaking moments. Today's culture molds the thinking of children and encourages them to have confidence in their own ability and emotions. This can be positive. However, understanding Philippians 4:13, "I can do all things through him [Jesus] who gives me strength," gives children identity in Christ rather than themselves. Relying only on self can be disappointing. Teach grandchildren to pray for courage and the ability to face problems. Knowing they are not alone will help grandkids throughout their lives.

> **Teach grandchildren to pray for courage and the ability to face problems.**

The apostle Paul tells us we have a responsibility to defend our faith. "Dear friends, although I was eager to write to you about the salvation we share, I felt compelled to write and urge you to contend for the faith that was once for all entrusted to God's holy people" (Jude 1:3).

Use prayer as a means to train grandchildren in relationship building with their Heavenly Father. God is not a vending machine. He cares deeply about every aspect of our lives. Model prayer like Grandpa Ken.

Grandpa Ken's Prayer

"Lord, I thank you for blessing me with all my grandchildren. Let me assist their parents in Christian training. Help me to discharge this responsibility humbly and faithfully by the strength of your Holy Spirit. Please make me an example of Christian devotion to all of my grandchildren. I thank you for your nurture and care in my daily life. Please nurture and care for my grandchildren. Give them the power to walk in the way of Christ. Please Lord, protect them from danger, grant them health, and grant them success in all their earthly endeavors. I pray this in Jesus' name. Amen."

BE A FAITH-FILLED ROLE MODEL

Scripture provides lots of role models for good and poor behavior. For example, have you noticed scripture says *honor* your father and mother? It does not say *love* your father and mother. Help your grandchildren by giving them reasons to honor *and* love you. When we honor all, we are honored. It's the Golden Rule: "So in everything, do to others what you would have them do to you" (Matthew 7:12a).

The Bible is filled with stories of those who walked alongside children, encouraging and supporting them. Paul mentored Timothy, a young man who impressed him with his great knowledge of God. "I am reminded of your sincere faith, which first lived in your grandmother Lois and in your mother Eunice and, I am persuaded, now lives in you also" (2 Timothy 1:5). Timothy's grandmother had a tremendous influence on her grandson. You can do the same for your grandchildren and other children. Are there young people you can influence, mentor, and guide as a surrogate grandparent? Step into young lives as an encourager. Knowing there are people who care makes a tremendous difference in the life of a child.

Grandpa Tom always blesses his grandchildren with the Aaronic blessing when they say good-bye to each other. He prays, "The Lord bless and keep you. The Lord make his face shine upon you and be gracious unto you. May the Lord lift up his countenance upon you and give you peace" (Numbers 6:24-26 NKJV). When Grandpa Tom was about to go into the hospital for surgery, his almost four-year-old grandson, Willie, called and blessed him in the same way. Grandpa Tom was incredibly touched.

How often do you hear an interview with someone you admire, only to discover his or her grandparents were a great influence in their journey, career choice, or faith in God? Some grandparents may never know the amount of influence they had on a grandchild (or, for that matter, anyone else). One may or may not be there to see the final harvest of the "seed of faith" planted in the fertile soul of a grandchild, but that is not the goal. The goal is for them to embrace faith in Jesus Christ, whether we witness the conversion or not.

Show grandchildren what it means to be Christian in words and actions. Grandchildren are watching how you treat people and if you choose to do what is right. Be the person who tells the clerk she has given back too much change rather than the one who brags about getting a bonus. And, let your grandchildren know not all people who claim to be Jesus followers act on Christian values. Discernment and honesty are attributes to be practiced. Grandparents can display their faith in Jesus in numerous ways; some are straightforward, and some are evident in encouragement and support. Find your own way to share and model your faith without being judgmental or demanding.

IDEAS TO APPLY

- ☐ Use the Bible as a tool for answers to your grandchildren's questions. Let them see you dig into God's Word.

- ☐ Talk about the Bible study you're participating in at church and explain how you see and live out the truth as found in scripture.

- ☐ Invite your grandchildren to special church events such as concerts, mission programs, and Sunday services.

- ☐ Text character qualities of Bible heroes to inspire godly choices. For example, you could text,

"Be a man (woman) after God's own heart.
Read 1 Samuel 13:14 and Acts 13:22."

❑ Participate in ministry service projects with your grandkids. Find such projects through your local church.

❑ Show evidence of your faith in your home (Bible, wall hangings, books, etc.).

❑ Wear Christian jewelry as an outward symbol of your faith in Jesus.

❑ Select a special prayer that you can teach your grandchildren. Recite the prayer together.

Dear Jesus, guide me today in all I do.
Let me show honor to others and you.
Be with our leaders and those I love.
Praise and thanksgiving, I give to you above.
Amen.

❑ Pray scripture.

"Search me, God, and know my heart; test me and know my anxious thoughts. See if there is any offensive way in me and lead me in the way everlasting" (Psalm 139:23-24).

❑ Study the Book of Proverbs with a grandchild. Select appropriate verses for your grandchild's age. Provide a notebook for your grandchild to record favorites.

❑ At Thanksgiving, give each grandchild a chocolate-filled Advent calendar. Choose a calendar that depicts a Christmas scene with Bible verses telling of the coming of Christ.

Explain to the grandchildren Advent is preparing for the coming of Jesus.

❏ Ask grandchildren to describe Jesus. Abuela Lorraine (Spanish for Grandmother Lorraine) loves Christmas and all the festivities. At Christmas, when all the grandchildren are gathered around, she asks one question before they open their presents: "Who is Jesus?" Over the years, she has been amazed and delighted with their answers. One Christmas, five-year old Mitchell said, "Jesus is the radiance of God." Abuela Lorraine was taken back by such an answer from one so young!

❏ Plan ahead for special faith-filled events. Grandma Nancy was in hospice care and knew she would not be around for the Confirmation of each grandchild, so she wrote each grandchild a special letter sharing her thoughts and prayers for them in the future. She attached a picture to each letter and asked her daughter to give the letters to the grandchildren at the time of Confirmation. Nancy is now with the Lord, but her grandchildren have a special message from her at the time they confirm their faith in Jesus.

❏ Make prayer a constant with your family. Paul wrote to the Thessalonians,

> "Rejoice always, pray continually, give thanks in all circumstances; for this is God's will for you in Christ Jesus" (1 Thessalonians 5:16-18).

❏ Say grace before meals.

❑ Pray for every grandchild and specifically for their future spouse every day. Let your grandchildren know you pray for them each day.

❑ Share with your grandchildren the analogy that prayers are similar to traffic lights. Some are answered with "Stop" (red), some with "Go" (green), and some with "Wait" (yellow). Often, it takes the passing of time to realize the real effect of God's answer.

❑ For years, on Christmas Eve, my (Carol) grandchildren put on a Nativity play for their parents and other guests. It was surprisingly fun and easy. No rehearsals needed! When the grandchildren arrived on Christmas Eve, each one decided which character to be and put on a corresponding costume simply made from pieces of oblong fabric. Mary was the most popular character, so the girls took turns. One of the older grandkids would read the story as the others acted out the play and proclaimed short, memorized verses. The play included some individual talents like singing or playing the violin or recorder. In the early years when the grandchildren were young, we always had a live baby Jesus, but later, we had to rely on a doll. One year, a three-year-old decided he wanted to be a sheep … and so he was! When the grandchildren got older, they wrote and directed their own amazing plays. Today, the grandchildren no longer put on a play; the celebration has appropriately moved on to other means of commemorating the birth of Christ. However, I know my grandchildren will remember the story of Christ's birth and the play. I often wonder if it will be revived sometime in the future. (I hope so.)

❑ As a family, volunteer at a charity. Many ministries encourage the whole family to participate in service projects. Feed My Starving Children, the Salvation Army Bell Ringers, and Operation Christmas Child are three of our (Carol) favorites. Service is a wonderful way to discuss the importance of being generous with time, money, and talents. There is nothing better than working side-by-side with a common goal.

❑ As a grandparent, volunteer to mentor young parents in your church, MOPS (mops.org), HIM4Her Ministries (Him4herministries.org), or other organizations. Your presence and wisdom are valuable.

❑ Volunteer in your grandchild's world. Consider vacation Bible school at church, school, camps, and mission trips. Assist, chaperone, make food, or make a contribution to help finance the experience.

❑ When a grandchild makes a decision to accept Jesus, welcome your grandchild into the family of Christ by sharing your faith story in written form as a legacy of faith.

❑ Sing with your grandchildren. Kids love to sing "The Johnny Appleseed Song" of thanksgiving.

> *Oh, the Lord is good to me.*
> *And so, I thank the Lord*
> *For giving me, the things I need*
> *The sun and the rain and the appleseed.*
> *The Lord is good to me.*
> *Amen*
>
> ©Kim Cannon & Walter Kent 1948

❑ Grandma Mimi has studied the Bible for many years and has personal notes written in the back pages of her Bible. One year, she made a copy of all the inspiring notes and gave each family member, including the grandchildren, a copy. Grandma Mimi's gesture shared the importance of God's Word in her life.

❑ Share your testimony of faith, tell your grandchildren why you love and depend on Jesus as Lord and Savior. Share your joy!

❑ Pray for each grandchild daily, by name, petitioning God on the behalf of the child.

❑ Kit Kat, my (Becky) grandmother, prayed each morning for her entire family by full name and birthdate. She claimed it kept her sharp and helped her remember each family member's birthday.

❑ Make religious benchmarks like First Communion and Confirmation special with a keepsake (cross necklace, bracelet, ring, Bible). A tangible gift will be a reminder in years to come of the life event. Include a letter of affection.

Great-aunt Ruthie was a major influencer in the lives of my (Becky) children. Her years of experience and first-hand stories brought depth to the tales she shared with the family. Aunt Ruthie was born in 1907. She walked miles to school with her siblings, went to church on Sunday in a sleigh with heated rocks or potatoes under her feet, and sold eggs from her little red wagon. At dinner one evening, my tween-age boys asked their great, great-aunt what the biggest technological advancement had been thus far in her lifetime. She thought for a few moments, then answered, "Watching the Mercury space mission. When the astronauts flew through the atmosphere and orbited the earth, I had to expand my thoughts regarding God and heaven. The Lord is bigger and mightier than I realized." Considering the advances in modern technology, such as cars, microwave ovens, and cell phones, it was fascinating to hear how science had magnified her faith.

APPRECIATION AND GRATITUDE

Things have changed in the way we express appreciation. According to many grandparents, the trend is moving away from formal thank you notes to a verbal thanks, a text message ... or sometimes nothing. The thinking is that a gift should be given with no expectation of a thank you note. The reasoning can be hard to understand for those of us who grew up writing personal notes of appreciation for every gift and kind action, including birthday, shower, and wedding gifts. You may have to alter your expectations in regard to handwritten notes, but you don't have to change your desire to teach and model gratitude.

Gratefulness kickstarts happiness! According to various studies cited by Harvard Medical School, "With gratitude, people acknowledge the goodness in their lives. In the process, people usually recognize that the source of that goodness lies at least partially outside themselves."[2]

Think of it this way in regard to thank you notes. The goal is appreciation for the time, energy, and money spent on the gift. Model appreciation for any effort or gift given to you. Thankfulness can go a

---

2   Harvard Medical School https://www.health.harvard.edu/healthbeat/giving-thanks-can-make-you-happier Accessed 02-33-21.

long way in teaching a positive life lesson to a grandchild. Showing appreciation completes the circle of giving.

IDEAS TO APPLY

> Showing appreciation completes the circle of giving.

❑ Teach your grandchildren to express gratefulness with, "Count your blessings one by one and see what the Lord has done." Help them name their blessings. A thankfulness journal is a helpful tool.

❑ Encourage your grandchildren to include thanksgiving when asking for the Lord's guidance. God's Word states, "Do not be anxious about anything, but in every situation, by prayer and petition, with thanksgiving, present your requests to God" (Philippians 4:6-7).

❑ Model your own appreciation for gifts with a note, call, or text message, encouraging grandchildren to do the same.

Gram has saved every thank you note her six grandchildren have sent her over the past 25 years. It's a testament to the power of appreciation and the written word.

Getting exactly what we want, precisely when we want it, leads to discontent. Consider our desire for instant gratification. We are all spoiled with modern conveniences: fast food, entertainment, shopping, and technology. Help your grandchildren learn patience and realize financial or behavioral limits benefit everyone. Patience, along with thankfulness, are virtues to which we should all aspire.

My (Carol) granddaughter, Ilsa, really wanted a computer ... a nice computer. She arranged with her parents and grandparents to have her birthday and Christmas gifts in cash. After two years of a few small presents to open, she was able to purchase the computer of her dreams. It was a lesson in delayed gratification.

HONESTY

Pontius Pilate asked Jesus, "What is truth?" Instead of waiting for an answer, he walked out (John 18:38), missing the answer from the greatest Messenger of Truth of all time, who only spoke truth and actually IS truth. In John 14:6, Jesus said, "I am the way and the truth and the life. No one comes to the Father except through me." This is the truth grandparents are called to instill in their grandchildren. "Fix these words of mine in your hearts and minds; tie them as symbols on your hands and bind them on your foreheads. Teach them to your children, talking about them when you sit at home and when you walk along the road, when you lie down and when you get up" (Deuteronomy 11:18-19).

Educating children in the truth is not a polite request from God. It's a command. Keep in mind, beating the ones you love over the head with the Bible is not the best tactic for embedding biblical truths into their hearts and minds. Leading by example, living by biblical principles, and loving like Jesus will get you much farther in leading your kids and grandkids to living a Christian life. "Jesus replied: 'Love the Lord your God with all your heart and with all your soul and with all your mind. This is the first and greatest commandment. And the second is like it: Love your neighbor as yourself. All the Law and the Prophets hang on these two commandments'" (Matthew 22:37-40).

Today, truth seems to be overshadowed. There's a pervasive attitude that "the end justifies the means," but the truth is, God cares about the process and the outcome. There's also often a willful denial of truth if it conflicts with one's personal desire. Holding a grandchild accountable to truth will benefit him or her later in life. This can be done with kindness and love rather than power, dominance, or intimidation.

Grandpa Buzz found he could share truth lessons with his grandchildren through his personal experiences. A favorite lesson began when he was waiting to start his career at West Point. During his six-month wait, he got a job at a local furniture store. He and a fellow employee were moving a sofa down some steep stairs at a home when it slipped and made a hole in the wall. He thought they should tell the furniture store owner, but his colleague said, "Absolutely not." So, they didn't. The next day, the owner came to him and asked if he had something to tell him. Buzz admitted what had happened. The owner told him the wall could be repaired, but his greatest disappointment was that Buzz did not come to him first with the truth. Buzz says he never forgot that lesson. For his entire military career and life, he took responsibility for his actions.

Be prepared for lots of grandchild questions about why you believe in God and rely on the Bible. "But in your hearts revere Christ as Lord. Always be prepared to give an answer to everyone who asks you to give the reason for the hope that you have. But do this with gentleness and respect ..." (1 Peter 3:15). Children are notorious for asking questions. "Why?" is a favorite for little ones. Answering with patience and sincerity builds connections with children.

Since grandchildren learn through questioning, give them a good reason to ask you questions. If you don't know the answer, say so and let them know you'll find an answer, and then be sure to get back to them. One good piece of advice about answering questions is to keep it simple and direct. Think: "Short answers for short people (grandkids)." Approach discussions and debates with God's wisdom from James 13:17a, "… the wisdom that comes from heaven is first of all pure; then peace-loving, considerate, submissive, full of mercy and good fruit, impartial and sincere."

My (Becky) grandma spoke volumes of love and faith into my life, as well as my siblings, and my children, too. The morning she passed away, I walked into her room and burst into tears. My eldest son, Ryan, wrapped me in a bear hug and assured me Grandma Kit Kat was having a much better day than we were. He knew where her eternal home would be, whom she would be reunited with, and the joy she would be experiencing in heaven.

IN SUMMARY: BANNERS FROM THE BLEACHERS
- Use the Bible to answer questions.
- Pray with and for your children and grandchildren every day.
- Happiness is related to both gratitude and goodness.
- Be a truth-teller.

CHAPTER 5

Connect the Generations

Grandma and Grandpa arrived for dinner one evening to chaos. The table wasn't set, the dinner was just beginning to be prepared, and homework was strewn all over the kitchen island. Their daughter, mother to the four grandchildren, smiled a weary smile. "I'm sorry we're not quite ready for dinner. The kids had soccer practice, piano, Cub Scouts, and book club after school today." Grandma and Grandpa jumped into the fray, helping with math homework and dinner preparations.

Families are *BUSY!* Unfortunately, there's not much "down time" in family life these days. Kids are involved in many more activities than when we were children.

AROUND THE TABLE

Mealtime with grandma and grandpa adds another whole layer of connection, tradition, and fond memories to the dinner table. Family stories, holiday traditions, and special foods can be shared around the table. The conversations are priceless. It's also a great opportunity to demonstrate the significance of gratitude in saying grace. Before dinner, the extended Larsen family would join together to sing either "The

Appleseed Song" or the Doxology. One evening, a three-year-old grandchild, Jaden, got so excited when he asked everyone to sing his favorite way of saying grace. All joined him in singing *"The ABC Song."*

> Mealtime with grandma and grandpa adds another whole layer of tradition and fond memories to the dinner table.

Why is gathering around the table for a meal important? It is the place kids learn many lessons including manners, communication skills, critical thinking, and relationship building. Sitting down at the table together offers family members an opportunity to share life with one another. Food is a natural draw for families. People have been gathering around the table for centuries. Unfortunately, family dinnertime is in fast decline with a 30% drop in the past 30 years according to the American College of Pediatricians.[3]

Mealtime is also a great opportunity to teach good nutrition. According to the American Academy of Pediatrics, there are significant nutritional benefits in family mealtime. "Children and adolescents who share family meals three or more times per week are more likely to be in a normal weight range and have healthier dietary and eating patterns than those who share fewer than three family meals together. In addition, they are less likely to engage in disordered eating."[4]

For generations, mealtime has been an intentional occasion to be together. Family meals build connections, including the extended family. The importance of dining together includes preparing the meal

---

3   American College of Pediatricians https://www.acpeds.org/the-college-speaks/position-statements/parenting-issues/the-benefits-of-the-family-table Accessed 02-23-21.

4   Copyright © 2011 by the American Academy of Pediatrics https://pediatrics.aappublications.org/content/127/6/e1565.full Accessed 02-23-21.

with grandchildren. Sharing recipes and cooking secrets for creating family favorites is entertaining for adults and children. And learning why families prepare favorite meals certain ways is fascinating.

You may have heard the story of a young bride who always cut off both ends of a roast before she put it in the pan to bake. Her husband watched and finally asked her why. She explained that was the way her grandmother always did it. Later, at a family gathering, the young husband asked the grandmother why she cut off both ends of the roast. She smiled and said, "Oh, I had to because I had a very small roaster pan. I had to cut it to make the meat fit in the pan."

Keeping meals healthy is good for everyone, but grandparents have a little sway when it comes to sweets and treats. A little girl was asked what her grandparents ate at their house and she replied with glee, "My grandmother and grandpa eat mostly ice cream and cookies, 'cause that's what they always have for me!"

When you add meal preparation and cleanup to time with your grandchildren, cohesiveness builds. Helping make, serve, and tidy up the kitchen after a family meal allows grandchildren to feel a part of the whole, a contributing member of the family unit. Even small children can help, so get everyone involved!

When I (Becky) was little, the females in the family were always informally assigned to the kitchen for cleanup after family dinners. I remember learning so much from my aunties and grandmas. They discussed everything from how to remove tough stains from tablecloths to why college was important for young women. All was learned with a dishtowel in hand.

IDEAS TO APPLY

❑ Write a cookbook with family favorite recipes. Add pictures and comments about the recipe … and the cook! Even a special recipe that's a family favorite and made time and time again can be forgotten in a matter of years.

❑ Preserving family recipes is a gift for generations. My (Becky) grandma, Kit Kat, was an awesome cook. Over the years, she wrote many recipes on darling recipe cards for me. As a gift for my mom, sister, and sister-in-law, I made cookbook pages with the recipes written in her handwriting, decorated the pages, and photocopied each one in color to create a cookbook of family favorites. The books can easily be replicated for each great-grandchild.

❑ Host a special dinner for your adult children, their spouses, and your grandchildren. Use a full set of china, even outdated pieces. Let the kids guess what little dishes (the bread plate or butter dish) above the dinner plate are for in a formal place setting. Try using finger bowls!

❑ One grandfather loved stimulating table conversation, but the grandkids just didn't seem too interested. He discovered if he wrote thought-provoking questions and let everyone at the table select one, the conversation just naturally evolved in an amusing and enjoyable way.

❑ Invite extended family for Sunday brunch or dinner. For consistency, select a regular time, like the second Sunday of each month, for example. If the date is on the calendar, families are more likely to join in the fun. Pizza Night is fun, too.

❑ Include a family activity with a meal.

❑ Think ahead to have favorite food items available for the unexpected arrival of a grandchild. One grandmother always has individual mandarin oranges cups and Oreo cookies handy. NOTE: Check labels for allergens if your grandchildren have any food allergies.

❑ Keep a list in a notebook or inside a favorite cookbook of what each family member likes to eat so you can plan menus accordingly. It's easy to forget and palates change.

❑ Create a personal kid cookbook with each grandchild. Let the child select what foods will be included. You might want to make sure there is a least one green vegetable … but it might not be spinach!

❑ Build manners into mealtime. Play act good table manners such as elbows off the table, hats off, and no talking with a mouth full. Teach the use of appropriate dinnerware and of course, asking to be excused. Make it amusing for the grandkids!

FAMILY HERITAGE

Who are you as a family? Sharing stories of those who have come before us gives children a feeling of lineage, heritage, and belonging. Tracing the family tree, hearing the adventures (and escapades!) of previous generations, and noting similarities between grandchildren and a loved one from the family tree, whether in actions or physical features, draws families closer.

My (Becky) kids adored my dad, Doc. He was a dentist, an artist in tooth restoration. My youngest son takes after his grandpa in artistic abilities. My mom and I see the similarities in Eric and Doc, beyond the art component. Their love of the outdoors, hunting, and fishing are the same. They both share a propensity for telling jokes and seeing the bright side of life. Looking at similar family member characteristics binds a family together. The following Ideas to Apply will provide a variety of ways to climb into your family tree with the grandkids!

IDEAS TO APPLY

❑ Create a simple photo album or photo collage with pictures of three or four generations to share with the grandchildren. Better yet, get the children to help design and create it. It does not have to be professionally done to tell the story. Use your printer for the photos, order them online, or print the pictures at a store kiosk.

❑ Teach your grandchildren a skill, hobby, or talent that you particularly enjoy. Get them on the golf course, fishing, or in the kitchen at an early age. It can make being with grandma and grandpa very special. My (Carol) grandson, Finn, is always willing to talk with his grandpa about the latest hot fishing spot!

❑ Share the stories of your family and tales of the younger days of your grandchildren's parent (your son or daughter). These stories will be told over and over and may even be requested for years to come.

❑ Create a "Funk Bowl" of family treasures and photos from all generations. Fill it with great conversation items such as antiques, special photos, ticket stubs, etc. The "funk" (old treasures) can be put in an empty fishbowl or any attractive container. You might decorate the container with a ribbon. The bowl becomes a three-dimensional family album and, when placed visibly on a shelf, also becomes a conversation piece. Anytime is the right time to put this together, but when grandma and grandpa move out of the family home, it's an especially good time to find such treasures.

❑ Print an annual calendar for each grandchild with photos of the family and acknowledge special family dates, including birthdays and anniversaries.

❑ The mother of five sons wondered what she would ever do with her carefully preserved wedding gown. When her first grandbaby was on the way, she had an idea. She talked to her son and daughter-in-law, who were thrilled with the plan, and went to work making a christening gown. Each subsequent grandchild was christened in the handmade gown cut from grandma's wedding dress.

❑ Do you live in (or could you visit) the community where previous generations lived? Plan a heritage tour with your grandchildren. Do some investigating: addresses, parks, churches, photos, whatever was part of the life of previous generations, maybe even the cemetery (depending on the age of your grandchildren). My (Carol) family did this, and with the help of some incredibly old photos, Keenan was able to match the photo to the home of her great, great-grandfather.

❑ Share the story of your courtship and marriage with family members. It's your own tale, but in a sense, it is also your grandchild's story. One little boy, after hearing his grandparent's courtship story, sweetly said to his grandfather, "I wish I could have been there."

❑ Bedtime is a great time for telling family stories. Plan ahead and think about the kinds of things you could share. Possibilities include stories of what it was like when you were young, having a telephone "party line", no cell phones, no internet, fruits and vegetables available only during the local growing season, television test patterns, only three TV channels (and no remote!), sock hops, and drive-in movie theaters. Younger grandparents may not remember these examples, but you will have your own remembrances.

❑ One grandfather, a veteran himself, feels strongly in sharing family stories of military service and sacrifice for our nation. He wants his grandchildren to know the enormous personal cost of freedom and liberty. Grandpa's favorite story to tell is of Uncle Ike who served overseas in World War I. Uncle Ike gave him his doughboy helmet. The helmet is now his grandson's treasure.

❑ Host a Heritage Draw by wrapping items, heirlooms, or old stuff that has been in the attic or a drawer. Let each family member select a wrapped item. Have more wrapped items than family members so if someone gets something they do not want, it can be turned in and another gift can be selected. Allow the family members to exchange items with each other if they wish. Share the significance of each item as it is unwrapped. Keep it light-hearted and fun.

☐ Adopted and foster kids are 100% family members. Help adopted family members find their biological heritage if they are interested. Locating and meeting biological family members is a choice. With the ability to research DNA and dig deep into family roots, many are finding pieces to their heritage. A number of online resources are available to assist in locating relatives world-wide.

A cautionary note, not all biological parents of adopted children want to be found. There are private reasons why mothers have chosen adoptive families for babies. Not all children desire to find their biological parents either. The choice usually belongs to the child. If the search ends in a dead end due to lack of information or lack of desire for contact, provide empathy and compassion. Reassure your grandchildren they are exactly where they should be, they belong to God and your family. Adoption is precious in God's sight! "God decided in advance to adopt us into his own family by bringing us to himself through Jesus Christ. This is what he wanted to do, and it gave him great pleasure" (Ephesians 1:5 NLT).

Cindy, never knew much about her biological family, only that she was either German or Russian. She did some searching as an adult but could only connect with her mother's family. Then she was given a MyHeritage DNA™ Kit and when the result came back, she discovered that she is primarily Irish! She now celebrates St. Patrick's Day with added joy because the celebration is part of her heritage.

GATHERINGS AND HOLIDAYS

Holidays and family gatherings can be an occasion for unity or a time of friction. Be willing to both compromise and share your personal preference. It's advantageous to plan ahead. Be considerate when planning family gatherings. Figure out the who, what, when, and where, allowing for all families to gather in celebration. Remember, distance, age, and the size of the family will all play a role in how family gatherings and celebrations happen.

After talking to a variety of grandparents, we discovered families usually work out their own schedules, meeting the needs of both sides of the family. But not everyone can have their first choice. Patience, fortitude, and compromise are needed. Only grandparents who had no control or did not state their choice seemed bitter to the process. Once a holiday schedule tradition is started, family members typically build plans around what they expect. Making changes needs to be done early, stated clearly, and with respect. One grandparent who has chosen to celebrate Christmas the week before the actual holiday, stated that it was a terrific choice for her family. She and her husband are no longer competing with their children's in-laws for time on Christmas Eve and Christmas Day. In addition, they are able to enjoy a quiet holiday, focusing only on God.

When planning family gatherings, remember each family has scheduling issues, extenuating circumstances, and individual concerns. Many times, it's hard to find the perfect time and date to get everyone together. As parents, we had years of hosting family events, coordinating schedules, and planning everyday activities, including holiday celebrations. Now may be the time to allow the next generation to take over, if they so desire. Let your kids know how you want to take part (foods, hosting, financially, serving in the kitchen, etc.), but be willing to allow for changes.

IDEAS TO APPLY

❑ When planning a family event, start in advance and give several options. Realize someone, or even an entire family, may not able to attend every gathering.

❑ Use an online calendar with dates for family plans. If all have access to the document, families can plan accordingly. If you're not comfortable putting your family calendar online, you can create a document and email it back and forth or pick up the phone to call or text.

❑ Host a quarterly family planning night with the extended family/families to talk about upcoming big events and dates.

❑ Combine holidays with the in-laws. This may be the easiest for your kids and grandkids so everyone can be together. Realize your child's in-laws are just as important as you and your spouse. If your in-laws or adult child/spouse prefer to keep holiday celebrations separate, then respect their choice.

❑ Plan an art or creative project to do over a long holiday weekend. This is a long-standing tradition in Grandma and Grandpa H's family. A highlight of Easter is an activity making dried empty eggshells into characters with a variety of feather, sequins, buttons, pins, and lots of glue. They used the decorated eggs for place cards the following Easter.

Holidays are a time for establishing family traditions, too. It is a time of gathering for the generations, a time to enjoy one another and feel connected. If you can celebrate together as a family, it's a plus, but if for some reason that is not possible, mark the holiday with a card, phone call or even a text message to your grandchildren on that day. You will want your grandchildren to know you are thinking of them. Remember, holidays are very important, especially to young children.

TRADITIONS

St. Lucia Day, December 13, is an important holiday in my (Becky) family. When Scott and I were married, my parents assumed the tradition would be over. What they didn't realize was the holiday was really special for me as well. Our tradition changed from me wearing a crown of candles, delivering breakfast to my immediate family to Scott and me driving to my parent's home with breakfast. Finally, the tradition changed to my family inviting Mom and Dad to our home for an early candlelight breakfast before the grandkids left for school. The tradition stayed the same; the logistics changed.

Taking turns, embracing new traditions, and combining family events are all options when your nuclear family changes. Traditions may have to be altered. Remember, each tradition had a "day one." Find new traditions that work well with your role as grandparent.

> Find new traditions that work well with your role as grandparent.

Traditions are passed down from one generation to another. As parents, we are accustomed to having the children home for the holidays and celebrating as we have in the past. It is kindness in action to remember your son-in-law (SIL) and daughter-in-law (DIL) have their own important traditions, too.

IDEAS TO APPLY

❑ Greeting cards can be very meaningful. Let your adult children (and spouses) know they are special by sending a card on Mother's Day and Father's Day.

❑ Grandma Sally had a tradition for celebrating birthdays. She would bake whole almonds in a birthday cake. Everyone loved the opportunity of possibly getting an almond to exchange for a shiny quarter. There was never any cake left over!

❑ Oma, Opa, and their family enjoy their own Thanksgiving tradition. They attend church together as a family. Afterward, some would go bowling while the cooks would do the final touches on Thanksgiving Dinner. The bowling winners get their names on a large, funky traveling trophy. It's become a fun, "competitive," family tradition. The cooking crew bonds over recipes and time together in the kitchen.

❑ Freja loves to gather together school friends to make lefse with her mother and both grandmothers. Put your own spin on baking Christmas cookies or decorating a gingerbread house with the grandkids and their friends. These activities can easily become holiday traditions. Be prepared for a messy kitchen and happy campers!

❑ Grandpa John wrote a detailed handwritten letter to his grandchildren each Christmas. He took notes on his calendar all year long, then composed the letters including national events, travel, school activities, sports, and personal thoughts. On Christmas Day, he read the keepsake letter aloud before giving letters to each grandchild. His grandfather and father had done the same. "The letters have been a wonderful history for our grandchildren of America and our family. We have lived a long time, so it's been great to have our history in a written form," shares his wife, Grandma Carrie.

☐ Grandpa Neil loves golfing and being with the family, so he combined both with a family golf scramble on the 4th of July. The course is usually not busy because families are gathering for picnics and other activities. When the tradition started, there were four teams and the youngest grandchildren loved riding in the cart and hitting the ball however far they could. Today, with older children and grandchildren, it is a competitive family tradition.

☐ Create a brand-new tradition. Consider interests, ages, and abilities or just pick something none of you have tried: mini-golf, archery, table tennis. Even if you don't repeat it, it will make a wonderful memory.

☐ Tweak an old tradition to accommodate the whole family.

☐ Family history includes national history. For example, study our American heritage and share stories lost to this current generation. Grandchildren need to know that WWII does not mean World War Eleven. Help kids understand the sacrifice made by many in the name of freedom. The idea that the United States was founded on a Judeo-Christian foundation is foreign to most students because it is omitted from modern textbooks. This topic is fertile ground for grandparents. The stories are fascinating, inspirational, and give a grandchild a true sense of national belonging.

Carol's family often participates in the 4th of July parade on Madeline Island in Wisconsin. Granddaughter Olivia has a 4th of July birthday. On her golden birthday (four years old on the 4th of July), the entire family carried signs saying, "Our daughter was born on the 4th!", "My sister was born on the 4th of July!" and "My granddaughter is an Independence Day baby!" Olivia wore a crown and rode her little bike down the parade route. All along the way, groups cheered and sang "Happy Birthday."

IN SUMMARY: BANNERS FROM THE BLEACHERS

- Mealtime matters.
- Be cognizant of the special family traditions and heritage you'd like to encourage.
- You can provide a feeling of belonging.
- Be flexible to accommodate the diversity of schedules.

CHAPTER 6

Plan Ahead

Five-year-old Xavier had been extremely anxious about starting kindergarten. His parents and Grandma Isabella read stories about school, visited the playground, and attended the kindergarten open house with Xavier to alleviate his fears. The first day of school arrived and he courageously climbed the stairs of the school bus and waved to his mama and grandma.

That afternoon, Grandma Isabella was at the bus stop, waiting for Xavier. He jumped down the last stair, ran into her arms, and exclaimed, "Grandma Isabella, you were right. Kindergarten was so fun! I'm glad I went today. Now, I'm done."

Grandma Isabella thought to herself, "Oh dear, he has no idea he has at least twelve more years of schooling to go." She took his hand, smiled, and asked, "Since you had so much fun at kindergarten today, maybe you could go back tomorrow."

Xavier looked up at Grandma Isabella and said, "Do you think I could go again? I had so much fun at school!" Grandma Isabella laughed and told her grandson she thought his idea to go to kindergarten again tomorrow was brilliant.

Grandma Isabella is one savvy grandma! Her response to her grandson's one day adventure at school prepared the way for yet another day ... and hopefully many more. Grandparents have an opportunity to gently lead children in the way in which they should go. Proverbs 22:6 reminds us, "Start children off on the way they should go, and even when they are old they will not turn from it." Thoughtful discussions and purposeful modeling are worthwhile gifts grandparents can give grandchildren. Time, listening, and compassion have great value. Money cannot buy heartstrings. But tangible gifts are meaningful, too.

GIFTS FOR GRANDCHILDREN

Birthdays are a special time to connect with grandchildren but often need planning with a capital "P." The day the child is born is a time for celebration for the entire family. There is joy in welcoming God's newest blessing. These festivities provide opportunities for connecting along with other occasions.

Significant life accomplishments of a grandchild can be applauded and acknowledged in extraordinary ways. Simple words of congratulations to unique gifts or adventures honor a child's achievements. Events in a grandchild's life, such as graduation, confirmation, and marriage, hold special meaning. It's a time for thanksgiving and remembering your grandchild is a gift from God. Determine your budget in advance, keeping in mind the total cost multiplies according to the number of grandchildren. Make it as fair as you can among all your grandchildren, even though it may not always be exactly the same price tag. Think ahead if you wish to give a family heirloom to mark the event or money to be used for college or vocational training.

For mile-marker birthdays, consider giving something more extraordinary. Here are a few questions to contemplate:

- What birthday year will be special, perhaps 10, 13, 16, 18, a Golden Birthday?
- What's the budget?
- What gift would be especially meaningful for each child?
- Is an adventure a good idea? If so, where and for how long?
- Is there a family tradition to incorporate?

IDEAS TO APPLY

❑ Give a small gift to open and money to save. Mimi and Poppy, grandparents of four, give each grandchild a wrapped gift for Christmas and birthdays. In addition, they give money toward the grandchildren's college accounts.

❑ Start small. One grandpa shared he had learned too late to begin with smaller, less expensive gifts. Never did he realize that as the grandchildren aged, the price of their gifts would increase, like going from LEGO™ to computers. Starting small gives one room to increase gradually.

❑ Grandma Bee always marked the day of a grandchild's first birthday with the gift of a "You Are Special and God Loves You" plate to be used on all future birthdays. You can find similar items at specialty stores or online.

❑ When grandchildren are in middle school or older, taking them to lunch at a restaurant of their choice and then shopping is a nice way to celebrate birthdays. When shopping, either give them cash to spend or choose an amount you're willing to spend. It can be a joy for both the grandparent and grandchild. A grandparent can learn a lot about the grandchild on a special birthday "date" and also what's trending!

☐ Collect dated items from the grandchild's birthdate or birth year. Coins, news magazines, and newspapers are ideas.

☐ Start a collection of mementos including school programs, special event bulletins, artwork your grandchild has made, sports programs of athletic events — all things that represent the grandchild's activities. Add photos, especially those taken with grandparents. Later, the mementos can be combined in a keepsake book and given to the grandchild at his/her high school graduation. If space is a consideration, consider taking photos of significant artwork and items your grandchild has created and compile them in a book or scrapbook.

☐ The tradition in my (Becky) mom's family was a special ring from the grandparents to commemorate the day each grandchild made a commitment to Christ. On the day I was confirmed, my grandparents gave me a delicate sapphire ring set in silver. Years later, my grandmother was happy to see it on my hand on my wedding day. The ring was my "something blue" and yet was so much more meaningful as a reminder of my grandparent's love at two life-marking moments.

☐ Gram has given each grandchild a monetary gift for high school graduation to be set aside to help pay for books the first year of college. The grandkids appreciated the generous gift, especially when they made their book purchase at the college bookstore.

❑ Older children are often happy with a gift card for a restaurant or gas station. Give an amount that makes you comfortable, it does not have to be extravagant. Your college-age grandchildren may like a gift card for a transportation service if they don't have their own vehicle.

❑ Check your local Christian bookstore or shop online for gifts for your grandchildren. An age-appropriate daily devotional is a wise and practical choice.

❑ Contribute to a charity or ministry in your grandchild's name. Choose a charity your grandchild understands or that the family already supports. Tuck something tangible that relates to the gift in the birthday card.

❑ A piggy bank is a good gift to encourage children to save their money and share with others. Include coins to get the savings started with a jingle.

❑ Handmade gifts are especially thoughtful. Sewing a quilt or making chocolate chip cookies from scratch takes time and energy. Homemade treasures are priceless gifts.

❑ Grandma Virginia loves to sew. One Christmas, she and Grandpa Alan gave the grandkids a play kitchen set. The kids loved the kitchen set but they kept borrowing food from the kitchen and often made a mess. So, Grandma Virginia found instructions for making food items out of felt. She made the grandkids felt hot dogs, cakes, pizza, cookies, and vegetables, so they could serve a beautiful make-believe meal out of felt!

❑ Grandma Judy found a pattern to sew a chef's hat and apron for Lincoln, her grandson, who at age two, loves to use his play kitchen set.

❑ Ask the child's parents to save old t-shirts from your grandchild's camps, sports, Scouts, and other activities. Sew a comforter, pillow, or even a skirt out of the shirts. If you're not a seamstress, hire it out!

❑ Create a traditional dress or costume for your grandchild depicting their cultural heritage. Many schools have Heritage Days or similar celebrations.

❑ Sew clothes for grandkids' American Girl™ dolls or other dolls. Patterns are readily available. Each American Girl™ doll has a storybook to inspire other craft ideas. Read the book together.

❑ Try woodworking. One granddad helped his grandchildren make simple photograph mounts. He used a 2" x 4" piece of wood, cut nine inches long. The grandkids painted their boards and mounted a clip to the middle top and attached a photo. The photo project stands on its own and can be proudly displayed on a table. NOTE: Be careful using power tools! Teach older grandkids the use of and care needed when working with power tools.

❑ Key into secret desires of your grandchildren. A grandpa knew how much his granddaughter wanted a dollhouse, so he built one out of scrap lumber. He even attached a small brass doorknocker to the front door. He enlisted help from grandma, who glued wrapping paper on the walls and made curtains for the windows.

"GRANDCATIONS"

"Grandcations" are special vacations with the grandkids that provide a wonderful way of creating memories. Finding the sweet spot can be challenging. Depending on the learning curve for the adventure, children need to be old enough to understand the educational aspects of the trip and participate in certain activities. The family calendar dictates the plan, as you will need to work around school calendars and activity schedules. Many grandparents have found ages 8-14 work well, depending upon the maturity of the children. Having fun and learning are both goals. "Grandcations" are a bit of "funshine" for everyone!

> **"Grandcations" are a bit of "funshine" for everyone!**

Here are a few suggestions with specific travel tips from a variety of grandparents. Cost and planning times vary. Many more ideas are available online at FaithfulGrandparenting.com.

KID-FRIENDLY PLACES TO VISIT

❑ Washington, D.C.
- Go online and find tours that are appropriate for your family.
- The "Monument Tour" is a must. If you know the name of a soldier who died in Vietnam, let

the grandchildren look up the name and find it on the wall. Explain the sacrifice made by all whose names are listed.

- Plan ahead to request tickets for a tour of the Capitol and the White House through your congressional representative.
- Purchase online tickets for the Bible Museum (useumofthebible.org). Make sure you purchase tickets for the short video tour of the District of Columbia.
- The metro city subway is an easy way to get around town, but a transportation service can be more convenient.
- Encourage grandkids to learn what makes our government unique. Give each grandchild a copy of the Constitution to read and discuss.

Grandma Mary Lou and Grandpa Roy took each grandchild to Washington, D.C., on his or her tenth birthday. It was a rite of passage in their family.

☐ The Creation Museum and Ark Encounter, Kentucky
Enjoy both the Creation Museum (creationmuseum.org) and the Ark Encounter (arkencounter.com) on a trip to Petersburg, Kentucky, just outside of Cincinnati, Ohio. Both are excellent and only 40 miles apart. Go online to determine what special events will be happening while you are there. Both are first-class, but the crowds can be large at peak times. Don't miss the planetarium!

❏ Disneyland™ or Walt Disney World™
Rise and shine early so you can enjoy an entire day at the parks. Make sure you investigate special events.

❏ Dude Ranch
Visit a dude ranch that is suitable to your grandchildren's age and your budget. The type of activities and riding facilities are considerations.

❏ Art Museums
Buy tickets in advance to save time and money. Grandparents often have different points of view from the grandchildren regarding artwork and displays. Discussions as to personal preference can be interesting!

❏ State Capitals
State capitals are great touring places with museums, sport fields, etc. One approach is to start local with your own state capital and branch out to neighboring states.

❏ Presidential Libraries
Delve into American history at the 14 presidential libraries in the United States. Create a Presidential Libraries Passport with a list of all the presidential libraries to encourage the grandchildren to have a goal of visiting each library.

OTHER KID-FRIENDLY ADVENTURES

❑ Fishing Trips

Fishing is a great bonding adventure! It also often teaches patience. Any lake is a good option for a day in a boat, especially when you include a shore lunch.

❑ Golf Trip

Consider taking your grandchild to golf school. Together, you can learn and improve your game. But better than that, you'll have a common interest and a shared experience. The local course is a convenient day trip. Mini golf is appropriate for all ages. Because of special golf adventures with Grandpa O, Aidan now shares his grandfather's passion for Natural Golf.

❑ National Park Camping

This activity takes some planning but gets grandchildren out in nature. Plan well with outdoor gear for sleeping on the ground. Renting or borrowing a tent-trailer with more modern conveniences is another option.

❑ Home Rental

Rent a home or cabin in a different part of the country or the world. Consider the desires of the family: beach, museums, hiking trails, golf, horseback riding, and more.

❑ Train Trip

Kids love train trips … short or long. If your grandchildren live in the suburbs of a larger city, they may find it a real adventure to take a commuter train downtown. If your kids live in an urban area, it may be adventurous to take them on a train trip through the countryside.

☐ Family Cruise
Cruise ships are fun for all ages. Due diligence is necessary in finding one that will work for your family. Look for cruise ship companies with activities for kids. Many cruises provide opportunities to learn about history or other parts of the world.

☐ Grand Camp Road Scholar
Learn about different trips you can take with one or more grandchild with the Grand Camp Road Scholar (roadscholar.org). The trips range in type, cost, and physical activity.

☐ Mission Trips
Take a church mission trip when the grandchild is old enough to participate. Serving others helps a child in understanding blessings and developing a grateful heart.

IDEAS TO APPLY

☐ Book a weekend at a hotel with a swimming pool. Young grandkids will like swimming and playing in the water. Normally, this is not too expensive and serves the same purpose as a trip without the cost of transportation to an out-of-town location.

❑ Grandma GG books a home on a lake each summer for her children and nine grandchildren. There are many activities for the grandchildren no matter their age. She uses this grandma/grandchild getaway as part of the Christmas gift for her adult children. She does the majority of cooking which gives the parents a special break. The following Christmas, she sends a simple book of pictures as a remembrance of the event with an invitation for the next summer.

❑ For big family gatherings, keep family members organized and on task during the "grandcations." Create a job jar using pieces of paper to write chores that can vary from helping with dinner, doing the dishes, cleaning up before bed, or even being the "herder" (the one with the whistle who gets everyone organized). Allow everyone to draw from the job jar for ways to help. Even a two-year-old can have a special chore like organizing the mess of shoes at the front door by matching the pairs of shoes!

❑ Enjoying nature at a lake cabin or hiking at a mountain cabin can be a great way to share the beauty of God's creation.

❑ Grandma T always had "Grandma Camp for Exceptional Children" at her lake cabin. She planned many activities, but most of all, they enjoyed the beach and water. Planning ahead for ever-changing weather, she included art projects, music, competitions, and board games with Grandpa T. A camp can be many days or just a couple depending on everyone's schedule. The grandkids cherish and remember those special times as Grandma T is now at home with the Lord.

❏ Grandma Sally has arranged many surprise trips, working with her adult children and spouses but not letting the grandkids know where they were going. She gave them clues and encouraged them to guess. She told the grandchildren what to pack and how long they would be gone. One of her favorite trips was to Milwaukee, Wisconsin, which included several hours by train. When given the clue of "riding on a train," one of her granddaughters was convinced they were going to Paris! They had a great time visiting the zoo, science museum, and all the sights ... in Wisconsin.

❏ Grandpa Tom takes each grandchild on a trip when the child turns ten. The grandchild gets to decide where to go and gives input on what to do. He has taken a grandchild to New York City, Montana, and Alaska. Each was a very special adventure.

Other ideas from seasoned grandparents will help you plan terrific outings for your grandchildren and keep things in synch during the expeditions. Subscribe to FaithfulGrandparenting.com for up-to-date adventures!

LEAVE A LEGACY

One of the more popular classes I (Becky) lead for parents focuses on legacy planning in regard to faith. Typically, I start the class with a question, "What legacy do you want to leave for your children and grandchildren?" It's been interesting to note that when thinking about a legacy in broad terms, not one participant in the classes has ever mentioned money or financial stability. The typical answers are happiness, good work ethic, healthy lifestyle, solid morals and values, cohesive family relations, good memories, and other intangibles. Money is a necessary part of estate planning and a practical way to provide for the next generation, yet perhaps not the most imperative. So, how important is money as a legacy?

The National Christian Foundation (ncfgiving.com) has studied this topic extensively and divides the legacy gifts for children and grandchildren into three categories:

1. Financial Capital — money, financial gifts, stocks, etc.
2. Character Capital — development, morals, and values
3. Spiritual Capital — development of a vibrant faith in Jesus

The NCF focuses on leading children and grandchildren to a place of "G.G.C." That is, generosity, gratitude, and contentment. They encourage grandparents to financially support activities and events that will have a lasting, positive effect on the next generation. By providing financial help to fund a camp, a class, a mission trip or outing, or even medical treatment, children will witness your desire to invest in their future.

Jesus stated, "For where your treasure is, there your heart will be also" (Matthew 6:21). What we value makes a big difference. Do you want your children and grandchildren to value a good work ethic, a lasting vocation, true contentment, and strong faith in Christ? Encourage sound values and positive traits including generosity. This is most effectively done through modeling, living out our words with definite action. Children do not always do what we say, but they always do what we do. Let your actions speak loudly.

> **Financially support activities and events that will have a lasting, positive effect on the next generation.**

IDEAS TO APPLY

- ❏ When providing finances for a camp, event, or activity, make sure the child has "skin in the game." Provide less than 100% of the fee or require some follow-up report, explaining that their commitment to follow through just might impact future gifts.

- ❏ Work with the parents regarding setting up a savings account for a grandchild, if you are providing a portion of the funding for getting it started.

- ❏ Show the next generation the joy of sharing by modeling generosity.

- ❏ Financially provide a parent getaway and be willing to babysit or hire a babysitter. This is a thoughtful gift for the whole family.

- ❏ Consider investing financially in your adult child's marriage. Too often, there is a great deal of money provided for a wedding and little for maintenance of the relationship. Marriage retreats are booster shots to keep a relationship strong.

- ❏ Providing grandchildren with financial help directly without going through your adult child and spouse is a recipe for conflict. Obviously, there are exceptions to this rule, but in general, discussions can save a great deal of anger and disagreement. No need to make yourself look good by slipping money to your grandchild. It's better to support the whole family and avoid undermining the parents.

Grandparents Jay and Sally give each grandchild an amount of money at Christmas. The grandchild can either match the amount or add to it, depending on age and ability, and generously give it to their favorite ministry. Then, at Easter, to follow-up, they gather together to hear how they used the money and how they felt about the process. It is a way of teaching generosity.

The goal is to treat each child the same way. However, for an assortment of reasons, that is not always possible. In the book *Splitting Heirs*, author Ron Blue says, "Love your children equally and as such, treat them uniquely."[5] This is important because each situation is unique.

Grandma Debbie took her oldest grandchild to Europe for a special graduation gift. However, the next three grandchildren were less than excited about such a trip. So instead, she gave a different, but equally special, gift to each of the other grandchildren. She never felt the gifts had to be exactly the same and tailored her gifts to the desires of each grandchild.

Use your time and finances to teach, direct, and encourage your grandchildren in healthy and productive lifestyles. This may mean there is less inheritance but more guidance. Ron Blue states it this way, "Do your givin' while you're livin' so you're knowin' where it's goin'."[6]

A legacy for the future consists of many aspects of inheritance including modeling and teaching money management, as well as possibly providing financial assistance. A financial planner can be of great help to you, your children, and grandchildren. Investigate

---

5   Ron Blue, *Splitting Heirs: Giving Your Money and Things to Your Children Without Ruining Their Lives*, Northfield Publishing: Chicago. 2004 p. 76.

6   ibid. p. 91.

simple things you can do to help a grandchild understand the value of money.

IDEAS TO APPLY

- ❑ A financial planner, no matter what the total value of your estate, can help you determine the best method of planning for your future and your grandchildren's future. There are many alternatives from which to choose.

- ❑ Help children learn the function of money by giving them an amount to spend on an outing. Let them decide if they want a souvenir to bring home or a special treat to enjoy on the outing.

- ❑ Hire the grandkids to do special jobs to encourage them to better understand the value of money and how money is earned.

- ❑ A child is never too young to learn how to manage money. One grandfather gives a children's book by Larry Burkett related to money management on the child's tenth birthday.

- ❑ Grandpa Ken said one of the first things he and his wife did when their first grandchild was born was to set up an education savings account. "We started a 529 Account and then relied on investment earnings to grow the money, tax-free, over the years. We moved the money once, to a professional investor with a variety of fund choices to manage the account. We thought it had substantial growth and were pleased. However, when our granddaughter was accepted into college, we nearly fell over when we saw her first tuition bill! The money in the 529 was barely enough to cover half of the first year's tuition. The cost of tuition had vastly changed over 17 years. With consecutive grandchildren, we made monthly payments into the account in addition to the interest income." NOTE: Check with your financial advisor before investing or making financial decisions.

❑ Open a financial TOD (Transfer on Death) stock account. The money will accumulate and be available for college, trade school, or a nest egg for the future. If the grandparent passes away, the child inherits his or her portion of the account. If the grandparent is alive, he or she can set the date for releasing the money to the grandchild. NOTE: Check with your financial advisor before investing or making financial decisions.

❑ Parents who set up financial accounts early on for their children will greatly appreciate any additional funds added by grandparents.

❑ Grandpa Rollie and Grandma Shirley left an inheritance for each of their four adult grandchildren with the stipulation that the money was to be invested, a nest egg for the future.

❑ Plan a yearly family meeting to share your thinking with the next generation. Whether your estate is large or small, the heirs will know how your estate will be transferred. Leaving it to the last moments of life can be distressing. Arguments and hurt feelings happen to the closest of families.

Grandma Trudy was a financial wizard. She taught her grandchildren a lot about money. She loved to check the stock market each morning before getting out of bed. She would place her trade, which was often successful, and then begin her day. One day, she heard her granddaughter say to a friend, with all sincerity, "My grandmother makes her money in bed."

LEGACY LETTERS

Legacy letters are about sharing your life story, passing on your personal history through words and photographs. The Apostle Paul wrote, "You yourselves are our letter, written on our hearts, known and read by everyone. You show that you are a letter from Christ, the result of our ministry, written not with ink but with the Spirit of the living God, not on tablets of stone but on tablets of human hearts" (2 Corinthians 3:2-3). In writing a legacy letter or ethical will for your family, you have the opportunity to impart values, stories, wisdom, and blessings. Let the legacy letter reflect your beliefs, experiences, and Christian faith. Include the many blessings you have received and your thankfulness to God. Your letter can be given to the family at various times during your life or left to be read after you have gone to be with the Lord. Point out the wonderful attributes of each family member and why each is special to you.

Generosity with loved ones includes time, compassion, and many other acts of kindness. Oliver Wendell Homes reflected, "Too many people go to their graves with their music still inside them." Share "your music"... your story and your treasures with those you love.

Share "your music"... your story and your treasures with those you love.

IN SUMMARY: BANNERS FROM THE BLEACHERS

- Commemorate special events in intentional ways.
- "Grandcations" are adventures for EVERYONE.
- Encouraging money management minimizes future financial woes.
- Take the opportunity to put down on paper your values, stories, wisdom, and blessings.

CHAPTER 7

Realize Times Have Changed

A grandma with a new smartphone was delighted to be able to text her college grandkids. Half the fun was adding a cute emoji to her messages. Unfortunately, what she thought was a smiling chocolate candy was actually a grinning pile of poop. Grandma laughed, so it became a funny family joke.

ACCEPT CHANGE

Do you remember floppy discs, Atari, or party lines? Your grandchildren more than likely do not. Times have changed ... a lot! Back then, marriage was considered a necessity before children, divorce was unusual, stay-at-home moms were the norm, pink was for girls, and blue for boys. Not today. In fact, your grandchildren may not understand the culture in which you were raised. Sharing childhood memories and a bit of the past can be a learning experience for them and a time to respectfully discuss why you believe the way you do. Sharing differences in opinion and experience may have a positive impact on the relationship with your adult children and grandchildren. Being aware of differences will help you discern potential difficulties and disputes.

Society has influenced parenting over the years; some is good, some is questionable. Most parents are open to suggestions. Children today are seemingly over-protected, but some of that is necessary because the world is different than it used to be. There are more perceived and real dangers. Adults desire to keep loved ones, especially grandchildren, in a bubble. Try not to be an overprotective grandparent. Allow your grandchildren to make mistakes and face consequences in order to be accountable and build confidence.

Who spends the greatest amount of time with our grandchildren? Who is influencing their thoughts and ideas? Many children spend a great deal of time with childcare providers, coaches, activity leaders, and other adults. Peers can also be very influential and yet, they are often lacking wisdom, maturity, and positive direction. A fourteen-year-old is not an expert of life yet but may still have significant influence. This can cause a detour from the traditional and moral values of the family. Dr. Josh Mulvihill, Executive Director of Church and Family Ministries for Renewanation (renewanation.org), studied the biblical responsibilities of grandparents to step into the lives of their grandchildren. "The Bible has many references to grandparenting, but they are often missed because the Bible uses phrases such as children's children, son's son, father's father, or forefather to speak about grandparenting. As you read three examples, pay attention to the responsibilities that God gives grandparents.

- 'Teach them [God's commands] to your children and your *children's children*' (Deut. 4:9).

- 'Fear the Lord your God, you and your son and your *son's son* by keeping all his statutes and his commandments, which I command you, all the days of your life, and that your days may be long. You shall love the Lord your God with all your heart and with all your soul and with all your might. And these words that I command you today shall be on your heart. You shall teach them diligently to your children ...' (Deut. 6:2-9).

- 'Tell to the coming generation the glorious deeds of the Lord ... which he commanded our *fathers* to teach to their children, that the next generation might know them, the *children yet unborn*' (Psalm 78: 4-8)."[7]

There are many examples in God's Word of how grandparents are essential in raising children for the Lord.

Children do truly listen to their elders (parents and grandparents) and do want to spend time with their family members. This is especially true for faith development. Research done by doctors Kara E. Powell and Chap Clark at Fuller Institute found children are most influenced by and connected to parents in matters of faith. The study concluded that parents ranked number one in the quality and quantity of faith support.[8] While parents have the

> Be comforted in the fact that most grandchildren do truly listen to their elders (parents and grandparents) and do want to spend time with their family members.

greatest influence on a child's faith, it's easy to see that an involved

---

7   Mulvihill, Dr. Josh, Renewanation: Helping Children Develop a Biblical Worldview. https://www.renewanation.org/post/understanding-the-biblical-role-of-grandparents. Accessed 02-23-21.

8   Dr. Kara E. Powell and Dr. Chap Clark, *Sticky Faith: Everyday Ideas to Build Lasting Faith in Your Kids* (Grand Rapids: Zondervan, 2011), 23.

grandparent's influence matters tremendously. Keep up the good work!

The role of grandparents will change as the grandchildren grow up. Families become busy and grandchildren become involved with school, friends, and numerous activities. It's easy to feel neglected, ignored, and angry. *Get. Over. It.* The truth is you are still extraordinarily important! Instead of feeling sad, abandoned, or no longer needed for babysitting and advice for everyday life, count your blessings. Realize how fortunate you are because your children have become self-sufficient and independent. Turn to prayer because prayer is a beautiful way to connect that is completely independent of them.

Sometimes Jan wonders if her grandchildren have any idea she once lived peacefully without a cell phone, that Roy Rogers was an enormously popular entertainer, and she witnessed the tearing down of the Berlin Wall, which was not in ancient times.

TODAY'S FAMILIES

Today's families look different from the past; they come in all shapes and sizes. Demographics and social mores have changed as well. This is a reality that grandparents have no choice but to accept. You don't have to like it, but the world is a different place now.

A 2015 Pew Research study identified specific changes in the current family structure. "Family life is changing. Two-parent households are on the decline in the United States as divorce, remarriage and cohabitation are on the rise."[9] Also noted in the study, "As a result of these changes,

---

9   Pew Research Center on Social Demographic Trend, December 17, 2015, Parenting in America, https://www.pewresearch.org/social-trends/2015/12/17/1-the-american-family-today/. Accessed 02-23-21.

there is no longer one dominant family form in the U.S. Parents today are raising their children against a backdrop of increasingly diverse and, for many, constantly evolving family forms."[10]

The diversity in family living arrangements can be contrary to what you had dreamed of for your child or grandchildren. Culture and media have made a mockery of traditional nuclear family values while claiming to be tolerant and open-minded. No matter what family system your grandchildren live in, you can be a source of stability and support.

And then there's the topic of sex. Opinions, thoughts, and privacy (or lack thereof) concerning sexuality have changed drastically in the last two generations. Today, young people look at sexual encounters differently. But remember, you are an influencer. Help your grandchildren plan for a future without the pain and stress that often comes from following the crowd and instead, assist grandkids in establishing a strong moral compass. Be willing to answer questions and discuss difficult topics, leaning into truth from scripture.

A young man asked his grandfather what he wore for sexual protection. The grandfather answered, "A wedding ring."

TAKE THE HIGH ROAD

Divorce, drugs, death, and desertion (the 4-Ds) are common maladies in today's world and are destroying families. Grandparents, your response matters! When one or more of the 4-Ds affect your extended family, your response will be a contributing factor in future relationships with your grandchildren. Our advice is to always leave the

---

10   ibid.

door open. Listen, respond with grace, and offer options and opinions when asked. Be supportive and err on the side of biblical and moral principles.

Grandparents are faced with a "double hurt" because they are empathizing with the grandchild *and* their own child. Hate breeds hate. As Christians, we are called to diminish hatred. Even in the worst of the 4-Ds, when your own daughter or son has been hurt in a relationship, make an effort to take the high road and be an example for the

> Divorce, drugs, death, and desertion are common maladies in today's world. Grandparents, your response matters!

grandchildren. Visible anger seldom improves the situation; consistent support does.

Sadly, your adult child may be the one who has made poor choices. Every person is responsible for choices he or she has made. While you can support and encourage, you cannot be ultimately responsible for bad decisions others make in life. Be available for your grandchildren and the caregiving spouse. Finding professional help is often the best approach in difficult situations dealing with infidelity, abuse, addiction, and other serious family issues.

TECHNOLOGY

At a birthday party for an 80-year-old grandfather, the guests were asked to tell of an amazing invention they had witnessed in their lifetime. The older guests remembered the first time they saw or flew on an airplane, watched television, drove a car with an automatic transmission, or used a digital phone. Toward the end of the sharing, a 16-year-old granddaughter said with a smile, "Well, I remember when I couldn't ask SIRI for help."

Advancements in technology and communication have brought significant changes and made life easier in many ways. But technology has also caused new problems and concerns. The computer saves a great deal of time, but when it goes down or isn't working properly, it's frustrating. The unreliability and inconsistency of online sources is another drawback. Not every website is truthful, trustworthy, or helpful. Some websites and social media platforms are damaging for grandchildren. Be watchful. When your grandchildren share an idea about something they saw online, ask questions about their online sources. Not all sources are reliable.

The great advantage of technology for grandparents (and everyone) is how easy it is to communicate with one another, wherever and whenever. We can connect not only by telephone and cell phones, but with email, voicemail, social media, text, and more. Messaging is terrific with grandchildren, especially with fun emojis. The beauty of today's technology is that you can keep in touch with grandchildren on their time without being invasive, and vice versa.

There is certainly a negative aspect to the technology world because it can also be addictive. Games and social media are tempting and can prevent face-to-face dialogue and communication. The ability to connect 24/7 can be both a blessing and a challenge.

A grandma told a humorous story of a grandchild's timing, or lack thereof! "My grandson was studying abroad in Europe and would text me with updates of his travels. Often, the text message alert would sound in the wee hours of the morning. He had forgotten he was six hours ahead of me, time-wise!"

So how does a grandparent handle cell phone use when face-to-face? A good tip is to encourage grandchildren to have a conversation without the distraction of a cell phone or other device. A frustrated grandpa made an "eyes on me when speaking" house rule, explaining to his grandkids that he'd prefer to see the color of their eyes when he talked to them. And adults need to do the same. Model good communications skills without distraction. In other words, put electronics down when your family is around.

> **Put electronics down when your family is around.**

An added benefit of having grandchildren and a computer is that they work well together! Kids can be a personal technology support team. Of course, the downside is they may look at grandparents as being "beyond help." Rely on your grandchild's expertise to set up the new computer, tablet, or cell phone. You will be successfully online with your new device and the "grand-tech" will have accomplished another technological feat, helping grandma and grandpa.

For example, one grandma and her grandchild made a mutually beneficial deal. Grandma taught Olivia how to knit and Olivia cleaned up grandma's hard drive. It was a win-win!

A savvy Grandma used this series as her voicemail message:
"Good morning. . . .
At present we are not at home but, please leave your message after you hear the beep. Beeeeeppp ...
If you are one of our children, dial 1 and then select the option from 1 to 5 in order of "arrival" so we know who it is.
If you need us to stay with the children, press 2.
If you want to borrow the car, press 3.
If you want us to wash your clothes and do the ironing, press 4.
If you want the grandchildren to sleep here tonight, press 5.

If you want us to pick up the kids at school, press 6.

If you want us to prepare a meal for Sunday or to have it delivered to your home, press 7.

If you want to come to eat here, press 8.

If you need money, dial 9.

If you are going to invite us to dinner or take us to a restaurant, start talking — we are listening![11]

TERMINOLOGY

Grandparent, BEWARE! With the evolution of communication, the English language has changed. Today, even the meaning of common words has changed. "Pot" is not just something you cook in, "hooking up" is not a good way to describe meeting a friend, and "sick" is not a description of one's health. Can you think of two definitions for grass, aids, chips, and hardware? Just for fun, and to be in the know, search online to find Webster's word lists. Research newly added words and the expanded definitions of old words. You'll learn that calling someone "phat" is a compliment! Fat is chubby, but phat is good-looking.

The same goes for acronyms. A grandmother wanted to express sympathy to a dear friend who had lost her husband. She sent a text and ended it with LOL, thinking it meant "lots of love." However, today it is more commonly known as "laugh out loud," NOT what she intended. If in doubt, check it out before sending a message.

Words can sound the same and be used in a sentence the same way, but the meaning can be misleading or different. Definitions of tolerance, racism, love, and rights have changed. This means that in order to have an open conversation, you must first have a clear

---

11   Beliefnet.com, https://www.beliefnet.com/prayables/galleries/funniest-grandparent-jokes.aspx?p=7. Accessed 02-03-20.

definition of what is meant by a particular word. This can be a learning experience for both you and your grandchild. The definition of words can differ from community to community and school to school, too. Since words have differing meanings, it's best to clarify.

ENTERTAINMENT

The entertainment industry is an enormous influence on our grandchildren. Television shows, movies, and music lyrics are speaking volumes into the lives of children. Talk to your grandchildren to learn what shows, movies, and music they like, and then listen together. Discuss the various aspects of the messages to gain insight on your grandchild's thoughts. Be wary and discerning of the values, morals, and stories told through media sources. Strike up a conversation and talk with your grandkids about what you've just seen and heard. Encourage them to think deeply and not just passively take it all in.

Dr. David Walsh, expert on media and founder of National Institute on Media and the Family and Mind Positive Parenting states, "Whoever tells the stories defines the culture."[12] Stories are a powerful source of identity, cultural norms, and societal values. Mass media has taken over the storytelling in society today. Often, the stories told are riddled with violence, sex, profanity, and a secular worldview. Dr. Walsh emphasizes this point, "… the average child will witness 200,000 acts of violence before he or she graduates from high school. This includes 20,000 murders. The real impact of this diet of violent entertainment, in my opinion, isn't just violent behavior. The most harmful effect is that it has created and nourished a culture of disrespect."[13]

---

12   Walsh, Dr. David, Spark and Stitch Institute. https://sparkandstitchinstitute.com/media-influence-whoever-tells-the-stories-defines-the-culture/. Accessed 02-23-21.

13   ibid.

Grandparents have an opportunity to turn the tide of disrespect, influencing grandchildren by assisting them in discerning the many aspects of media, both positive and negative. This includes movies, television shows, online games, and news programs. Help grandchildren separate fact from fiction, fantasy from reality, by asking questions about what they are watching.

Help grandchildren separate fact from fiction, fantasy from reality.

Rather than choosing to watch stories of others on the big screen, share stories that matter to your family. Hearing stories, watching family movies, and looking at photos of generations past are all activities that ground grandchildren. Children will realize they belong to an extensive family tree and a story that is bigger than just themselves.

Share the stories that matter to your family.

IDEAS TO APPLY

❑ Music is a generation connector. Share your favorite musicians and styles of music with the kids. Who knows, they may learn to love the music of Frank Sinatra, Charlie Pride, or Gladys Knight! And for you younger grandparents, Bon Jovi, Journey, or Amy Grant.

❑ Ask your grandchild the name of his or her favorite musician. Then learn to identify the music and maybe even memorize the lyrics of a song. The kids will be impressed!

❑ Request the grandkids put together a multigenerational playlist.

❑ Christian music not only encourages the love of music, but also the love of the Lord. Even if your grandchildren do not go to Sunday School, you can witness to them through hymns and contemporary Christian music.

❑ Use reputable, Christian, online movie review sites (pluggedin.com and movieguide.org) to decide what media venues are acceptable.

Grandma chuckled as she heard the story of her middle school grandson hopping in the car one day and sharing his "new" favorite song with his mom. He was horrified when Mom started singing along. Unbeknownst to the kid, the song was also popular when she was in middle school. Journey's classic hit, "Don't Stop Believing," is evidently timeless.

IN SUMMARY: BANNERS FROM THE BLEACHERS

- Roll with the changes because families come in different sizes and shapes.
- Embrace technology and use it to connect.
- Rely on tech-savvy grandchildren.
- Use family stories to entertain and delight grandchildren.

CHAPTER 8

Acknowledge Possible Challenges

Grandmother was very disappointed when she saw her granddaughter, Keatyn, kick her younger brother. She gently pulled her aside, explained why kicking was hurtful, and how she never wanted to see Keatyn behave like that again. She then asked Keatyn what she had learned from their conversation. She thought for a moment and responded, "Pull his hair instead of kicking him?!?"

What are the greatest challenges in grandparenting today? According to a vast number of grandparents, the challenges are as complex as the families. And yet there are similarities in some of the common challenges. We'll explore the difficulties and provide ideas to overcome obstacles to intentionally connect and build strong relationships.

DISCIPLINE

Approaches to parenting change with every new expert in the field. The "right way" to discipline is a moving target. Model respect concerning how your adult child is choosing to raise your grandchildren.

Keep in mind, you were a brand-new parent at one time, navigating the best you knew how.

A grandma was listening to a group of younger women sharing anecdotes on parenting.

One said, "Oh, the twos are the worst!"

Another young woman added, "School age is definitely harder."

A third woman laughed and said, "You're both wrong, teens are the worst!"

With that, the grandmother smiled and said, "Just wait until your child turns 42."

In the area of discipline in your home, it's appropriate to have your own house rules. Know that "the playbook" for behavior and attitudes at grandma and grandpa's home can be different than the rules your adult children and their spouses have at their home, and that's just fine. You had rules and expectations for your own children while they were living under your roof. Your grandchildren will actually benefit from specific rules to guide behavior while with you and in your home. It's good for grandchildren to learn that house rules can vary by home and respect of the house rules is important. Establishing the house rules early will be good for both you and your grandchildren.

Grandpa JJ and Grandma often watch the grandkids in their home. They learned quickly to set some ground rules with both the parents

It's appropriate to have your own house rules for behavior.

and the grandkids. They determined the first course of action was to discuss the house rules because they knew their grandkids would try to fudge on the rules, "just a little." Deciding on bedtime, routines, and use of cell phones were included in the house rules.

Safety and polite behaviors are topics to be addressed as well. Write down and post your "House Rules." Grandkids adapt to different standards, but they also test rules. Be the grandparent that cares enough to enforce the house guidelines with logical consequences.

Kids love to negotiate! Don't be afraid to use the standby, "Because I said so," followed up by "This is my house. I get to choose the rules." Too many explanations often cause great debates. Once a negotiation begins, it rarely ends well. State your expectation or directive and move along accordingly.

In your "House Rules" playbook, phrase the guidelines in a positive way. Keep in mind, the rules will need to be updated as the children mature. Depending on the age of the children, you can interject some humor and still get your point across. Here are some suggestions of possible rules for your home.

> **Be the grandparent that cares enough to enforce the house guidelines with logical consequences.**

HOUSE RULE	HOW TO SAY IT IN A POSITIVE & FUN WAY
Hats off when eating.	At the table, we love to see you, not your hat.
Swearing is not allowed.	Be kind and gracious with your words.
The dinner table and all bedrooms are tech-free zones.	All electronics are to be locked up in Tech Jail at mealtime and bedtime.
Don't be rude to Grandma and Grandpa's friends.	When meeting your grandparents' friends: Shake hands, look in the friend's eyes, and speak a greeting like, "It's nice to meet you." Greet adults politely.
Remove shoes when entering the house.	Your shoes would like to stay on the mat by the front door.
Come to dinner when called, the first time.	When dinner is called, wash your hands and hurry to the table.
Clean up your own mess, including dishes at mealtime.	We fired our maid! Everyone cleans up after themselves, including clearing the table after a meal and helping with dishes.
Ask before turning on the television or computer.	Plead your case if you want screen time. Grandma and Grandpa control the remote and mouse.
Loud voices and wrestling are for outside play.	Loud voices and roughhousing are fun OUTSIDE.

What are logical consequences for not following your House Rules? This is where talking to the parents of your grandchildren is important. Some parents are happy to have grandparents handle discipline within their own home, but some are not. Ask for suggestions in handling poor behavior. Discuss options and give your opinion on consequences and punishment. And then, if possible, follow their lead and respect their wishes. Use discretion and common sense to set and enforce the limits and do so with respect. Make the consequences of misbehavior known to your grandchildren so they know what to expect. Err on the side of being fair and consistent.

Confusion comes when a grandchild misbehaves in your home while the parent is present. Who is responsible for discipline? Grandpa says, "It is my house." The parent says, "It's my child." Work together and back each other up for the good of the child.

> Err on the side of being fair and consistent.

GRANDCHILDREN MILES AWAY

When your adult child settles far from their hometown and your grandchildren arrive, it's difficult! But you might be surprised at how connected you can become with grandchildren that live miles away. Most importantly, let them know you desire to intentionally connect. Plan ahead for visits.

With the COVID-19 pandemic, many families were separated, not by distance but by the virus. Grandparents have found creative ways to connect with their grandchildren regardless.

> You might be surprised at how connected you can become with grandchildren that live miles away.

Online platforms for face-to-face conversations, doorstep deliveries of homemade treats, and virtual birthday parties are a few innovative ideas grandparents have used to keep in contact with extended family.

Alan is a grandfather who becomes frustrated when visiting his out-of-town family. For him, there's always too much chaos in the busy household. He and Grandma Ginny solve that problem by staying in a nice hotel with a swimming pool. It is a win-win for everyone. The grandkids love visiting and swimming. The grandparents can say goodnight and wrap things up on their timeframe.

IDEAS TO APPLY

☐ Nana Judy, who lives far away from her nine-year-old granddaughter, started a "Book Club" with her. Granddaughter Kenley selected the book, *The Wishing Tree*. They both read it. On Sunday nights, they discussed the book and plot via Skype. A year later, her grandson, Brecken (Kenley's younger brother), requested his own "Grandparent Book Club." He and Grandfather Don are making plans to connect.

☐ Send surprises. Grandma Peggy, a widow with little ones far away, sent a surprise box to her grandchildren every two or three months. The boxes contained age-appropriate gifts she knew would bring pleasure to the grandkids. Her daughter-in-law informed her that Stella, at age two, would recognize the box and grab hold of it with great delight.

☐ Use Facetime or Skype to connect with far away grandchildren.

- [ ] Text a "photo a day" to your grandchild and ask the parents or older grandkids to send one back to you.

- [ ] When visiting the grandkids, bring a treat for the family pet. Lady, the beagle, loved to see Grandma arrive because she would get her favorite dog biscuit.

- [ ] Bring your own "show and tell" items when visiting the out-of-town grandchildren. For example: souvenirs from your latest trip, the sweater you're currently knitting, photos of the grandchild's parents, or a game to play together.

It's smart to take advantage of technology to enjoy being connected to the grandchildren in your life! There are a number of excellent ways for grandparents who live far away to have face-to-face time with grandchildren. Set up a time each week to connect. Continue to investigate other modes of communication; it seems there's something new every day!

Grandma Mary often used Skype to talk one-on-one with her grandchild. Just before a real visit, Mary's adult child (the mom) told the grandson that grandma was coming. Immediately, the little boy ran over to the computer to see grandma, who, according to the grandchild, lived in the computer.

There are two big advantages to having grandkids far away. First, you can schedule your visits and know you are dedicating time to the family. Second, you get to see and take part in family life in their surroundings, especially if you stay in their home. Many of the ideas and suggestions in this book can easily be applied to the relationships of grandchildren next door or miles away. However, grandchildren who live some distance away require extra planning.

ABANDONING THE FAITH

There is no greater joy than knowing your children are walking in the truth of God's Word (1 John 1:4). However, today many children and grandchildren have turned away from faith, church, and the Christian worldview. Children may accept and live by their parent's moral teachings and principles but miss the very foundation of Christianity, Jesus. They have chosen to follow a secular worldview, which can be very enticing because it's glorified by today's culture.

Keep praying that doubting grandchildren will find Christ. If children openly express doubt, let them know everyone has periods of doubt. Encourage the study of God's Word to realize truth in the Bible and its gift to all who embrace it. As a grandparent, do not get discouraged. Keep praying, encourage Bible literacy, and most of all, hold on to the promise of Christ and entrust your loved ones to him.

Encouraging children and grandchildren in faith-building activities like attending church, reading the Bible, watching Christian movies, and taking part in faith-based mission activities can do a great deal to plant seeds of faith. Even if children know the stories of the Bible, the foundation may be missing. Knowing who Sampson, Moses, and Goliath are doesn't mean the truth behind the stories is embedded in a grandchild's heart.

Hold on to the promise of Christ and entrust your loved ones to him.

Dr. R. Albert Mohler, Jr. writes, "Parents are to be the first and most important educators of their own children, diligently teaching them the Word of God (Deuteronomy 6:4-9). Parents cannot franchise their responsibility to the congregation, no matter how faithful and biblical it may be. God assigned parents this non-negotiable responsibility, and children must see their Christian parents as teachers and fellow students of God's Word."[14] All grandparents are fellow students as well, growing and encouraging Bible literacy in all generations.

EXPECTATIONS

Expectations can drive emotions, especially in our desire to spend time with the ones we love. Unfortunately, busyness has become a badge of honor in our culture. Grandparents can become frustrated at times, especially when grandchildren become increasingly busy with everyday life. As a result, they have less time for grandparents and family events.

Sometimes our expectations need to change. One grandma was determined not to expect much in the way of inclusion in her grandchildren's lives. Because this grandma was familiar with the Alcoholics Anonymous goal of keeping realistic expectations, she simply transferred that idea to grandparenting. She realized the younger generation would have commitments and plans that may not include her. With realistic expectations, she could be more often surprised and happy with the way events unfolded in her interactions with her grandchildren.

Busyness can be hurtful but is normal. Don't allow hard feelings about this separation to fester. Differences in interests and activities can make grandparents feel left out. Learn to enjoy the coming of age of the next generation by listening and being attentive.

Not long ago, a group of grandmothers were sharing stories of their grandchildren. One grandmother told a story of a grandchild

14   https://albertmohler.com/2016/01/20/the-scandal-of-biblical-illiteracy-its-our-problem-4/ Accessed 02/23/21.

who faced great challenges and as a teenager has become an overcomer. Grandma had encouraged and prayed for her grandchild during this difficult time. With a sweet smile, the grandmother admitted, "Oh, how I wish she were young again and wanted to be with me rather than her friends all the time."

Another grandmother told of her grandson coming to their home and announcing to his grandparents that he still liked them, but he would not be spending much time with them anymore. He informed his grandparents, "I have my own friends now." Ouch!

This transformation can be painful, but it's also a positive. Children are totally dependent when they are young. Independence is encouraged. When children do branch out on their own with new relationships and activities, they need room to spread their wings. Interdependence blooms as they learn to rely on others for assistance. The goal is to ultimately become dependent solely on God. The stages vary in each child and are not linear. Celebrate these stages and cheer your grandkids to the goal: personal faith in Jesus Christ.

Communicating and fitting in with lifestyle changes can be challenging, too. Grandparents can at times be at a loss when listening to the conversations of the younger generations. Try to keep up with current trends and terminology to be in the know on the latest and the greatest.

Grandmother Oma commented that at family gatherings she sometimes thinks she is in a foreign county because the family members seem to be speaking another language when discussing the latest trends in entertainment, fashion, and technology. Her answer to the "language barrier" is sweet. She laughs and says, "I guess I need to study that new modern language." She's being proactive in the relationships with her grandchildren.

Sometimes the old ways are ignored, and the new ways may seem strange. Do your best to get on the same page while at the same time sharing your perspective. Grandchildren can feel alone, too. Let your grandchildren know you are willing to listen and will try to understand and help them do the same. Respect is a two-way street.

PHYSICAL LIMITATIONS

Not only do your grandchildren change over the years, but so will you. Challenges come with age: a loss of energy, a concern about driving after dark, and maybe even a loss of memory. Make sure you share your limitations with your grandchildren so they will understand why you no longer can travel 15 miles in the dark for their 7:30 sports game.

> **Make sure you share your limitations with your grandchildren.**

A grandmother was alarmed to discover that occasionally she would toot (pass gas) when she stood up. The grandchildren found that to be very funny and would giggle. She decided to confront the embarrassment by laughing right along with the grandchildren and announcing, "Just call me Grandma Tootsie. I make music!" They all laughed together.

If you deal with hearing loss, let the kids know! Rather than taking a backseat in the conversation, ask the grandchildren to please look directly at you and speak up. Feel free to ask them to repeat something if you don't hear it the first time. This may seem annoying, but it shows you care enough to want to know what they are saying.

The same goes for other physical limitations. Wheelchairs, scooters, canes, and walkers are ways some grandparents get around and keep moving. Our bodies may be aging and slowing down, but we can still be young at heart! Show your grandchildren how the various mechanical aids work and allow the kids to help you.

STRETCHING THE DOLLAR

Financial challenges for grandparents are common at retirement when the salary ends, and the income is fixed. Think through ways to be creative without spending a lot of money. Simply acknowledging the child by listening and caring deeply has tremendous value, and doesn't cost a thing.

IDEAS TO APPLY

- ☐ Taking grandkids to a restaurant can be very expensive, especially if you have many grandchildren. Grandma Gloria, a cost-conscious grandmother, set expectations early on by telling the grandkids they could have water or milk at restaurants, no kiddie cocktails or soda pop. She claims it's amazing the amount of money she saves and that's why she's able to take the grandkids out as often as she does.

- ☐ Many grandparents find great treasures from dollar stores or garage sales. Name brands are wonderful, but funny and silly items can be equally enjoyable.

- ☐ One grandfather sets a dollar limit on gifts and gives it to his adult child and his/her spouse to purchase an appropriate gift for the grandchildren. With this approach, he feels the grandkids are given something they really want, and the money is wisely spent. However, one time, the parents purchased necessary items for the grandchildren (socks and underwear) and from that point on, the grandkids were never too excited to open presents from grandpa! Setting some expectations with the parents can be helpful.

- ☐ Take your grandchildren to a movie midweek when movie prices are usually better, especially for seniors.

- ☐ The public library is a great resource. Take the grandkids to storybook hour or other events. Make sure the topic and book are appropriate. Pre-read books for young children.

- ☐ Most children love puppies, kittens, or fish at the pet store. The hard part is leaving the store without a fuzzy friend, but a promise to return to the store usually is sufficient.

- ☐ Plant a garden with your grandkids. If space is a consideration, make container gardens.

- ☐ Nurseries and arboretums offer fun excursions, activities, and special events.

- ☐ Bike rides and parks are fun for everyone. Teach the grandchildren how to read a trail map. Give them the choice of parks and distance of a ride. The type of bike and distance will depend on the age and ability of the grandchild (and you). Bring treats from home.

- ☐ A grandpa suggested his "every holiday gift-giving" wife keep grandchild gift giving under control. Not every holiday needs a special gift. A handwritten note, a card, or candy bar might just be enough. Possibly give a surprise gift during the year, a present the grandchild really needs or wants. Keep track to be as fair as possible with all grandchildren.

Grandma GG has nine grandchildren and is somewhat limited in the amount she can spend on each one. She opened up nine savings accounts at her bank, one in each grandchild's name. At Christmas and birthdays, she puts $25 in each grandchild's account and sends a personal note to the grandchild, showing the dollar amount in the account. She started when the grandchildren were young, and by the time they graduate high school, each account will accrue to more than $1,000. It's also fun for the grandchildren to watch their accounts grow. She is modeling how a little bit saved over time can add up to a lot (depending on interest rates).

FRACTURED FAMILIES

If your adult child and his/her spouse are separated or divorced and your grandchildren are living with the parent who is not your child, it can cause many difficulties. Be encouraged! There are a multitude of possibilities for connecting with your grandchildren. The custodial parent, whether your adult child or not, is often in need of help with babysitting, transportation, or maybe home-cooked meals. Find out where you can be of assistance. Work to build relationships. Even if your adult child and spouse have an estranged relationship, yours may not have to be adversarial. While you don't want to undermine your adult child, there may still be a role for you to play as grandparent.

Some fractured families are estranged with little or no contact with other members of the family. For a grandparent, this can result in being separated from grandchildren as well. This topic of estrangement is often taboo because of embarrassment or even willful denial. Estrangement is kept in the shadows but can cause great pain. Karl Pillemer, Ph.D. sociologist and professor at Cornel University determined it is a "silent epidemic" because many families experience estrangement but keep it hidden. In his book, *Fault Line: Fractured Families and How to Mend Them*, he stresses that families need to know they are not alone. Dr. Pillemer's book contains original research, individual stories, and case studies of how estrangement and reconciliation can be dealt with proactively. No two paths are the same, but each begins with the desire to end the estrangement and restore the relationship. In regard to arduous family relations and estrangement, Dr. Pillemer offers this advice, "If you have a relative desperate to reconnect, offer one last chance: If you are offered one last chance, take it."[15] There's wisdom in offering and receiving grace.

Don't put off the need for reconciliation with a family member by thinking, "I will do it next month (next year)." One never knows when the opportunity will run out. Recently, a good friend had a sudden brain bleed and her life ended. The pain and agony the estranged adult son showed over the strained relationship with his mother was heartbreaking. I (Carol) know my friend loved her son, but I am sure she kept thinking if she waited long enough, her son would be the first to approach her for reconciliation.

TRYING RELATIONSHIPS

Family dynamics change. Daughters-in-law and sons-in-law become members of your family. Plan ahead regarding how you want

---

15   Karl Pillemer, Ph.D., *Fault Line: Fractured Families and How to Mend Them* (New York: Penguin Random House, 2020), 244.

your relationship with them to be. Think back to when you were first married. How did your new in-laws treat you?

- If you were blessed with a loving, respectful relationship, it was a gift. You have a positive model to use in how you relate to the person your child has chosen for a mate.

- If love or even "like" were missing from the bond with your in-laws, contemplate how you can relate differently. How can your negative experience be turned into good for your child's spouse and the family?

The Bible provides the answer. The Book of Titus gives positive directions to older women to be reverent in the way they live, to teach what is good, and to urge younger women to love their husbands and their children as well as be self-controlled. Grandmothers are called to be the older woman who shows kindness and understanding, even in difficult times (Titus 2:3-5). Grandfathers are to be role models in "being temperate, worthy of respect, self-controlled, and sound in faith, in love, and in endurance" (Titus 2:2).

Why is there so little common grace between in-laws? Is it fear of not being in control, resenting the intrusion, feeling a sense of competition, holding to different thoughts or opinions, or just plain dislike? Whatever it is, it's uncomfortable for everybody.

A parent educator tells the story of teaching a class of young mothers. She was so impressed with the young mothers and their desire to provide the very best for their families. They wanted to do what was right to help and encourage their children. However, the one area that really surprised her was the irritation and contempt many seemed to have for their in-laws, especially mother-in-laws. She heard one story after another and noticed an unpleasant spirit. She questioned if their concerns were founded or not? She felt she certainly could not judge their feelings or their actions. During the class, she was determined to help restore broken relationships by encouraging the mothers to extend kindness and forgive.

In-law and other family relationships can be hard, because intended (or unintended) comments and actions can sometimes be very hurtful. It rarely helps to demand attention or appreciation. Committing to respect the person your adult child has chosen to marry may be difficult. How you respond will determine the connection you have with your in-law and ultimately, your grandchildren.

After talking to grandparents and parents, it is clear that each family is different. Accepting and appreciating differences is helpful. Usually, the mother sets the tone for the family and so the adage, "A son's a son until he takes a wife, and a daughter's a daughter all her life," sadly holds a bit of truth. But understanding that each family establishes its own tenor can be a step toward harmony. Unfortunately, some relationships will always feel like "walking on eggshells."

When Grandmother K was asked if she had any advice or ideas to share with other grandparents, she jumped at the chance. She quickly said she regrets the years she resented the "other grandmother" who sometimes seemed like a second mother to her grandchildren. She felt left out and rejected. But now she has changed her mind and thinks differently. She wishes she had been appreciative of what the other grandmother was doing for the grandchildren, rather than being jealous and angry. Her grandchildren are now grown. Grandmother K and her husband have a delightful adult relationship with the grandchildren, for which they are grateful.

For many, family is the most important part of life. For those who do not have a good relationship with extended family members, it just may be time to be bold, apologize, and search for how best to work with family members. Consider cutting an even wider path of forgiveness and humility.

> **Consider cutting an even wider path of forgiveness and humility.**

God's Word has a lot to say about forgiving others. Jesus covered many topics, including forgiveness, in the Lord's Prayer. Scripture is direct about the topic of forgiveness, "… and forgive us our sins, as we forgive those who sin against us" (Luke 11:4a NLT). If you're the one who has created friction in the relationship, follow the Lord's lead, ask for forgiveness, and let it go. Sitting in guilt and remorse isn't good for anyone. Put the situation behind you and move on. "Therefore, if anyone is in Christ, the new creation has come: The old has gone, the new is here" (2 Corinthians 5:17).

Unfortunately, although you can forgive, you may not be forgiven. Reconciliation is the goal, but it is not always achievable because it's a two-way street. Pray God will work in hearts to heal the relationship in due time.

Martha shared that her relationship with her daughter-in-law (DIL) was very difficult. They both had made unintentional, hurtful comments. The tension in the relationship was unbearable. This humble grandmother decided to change the situation by serving her DIL as a surprise helper. Once a quarter, she would do something unexpected, such as send flowers, provide food, or purchase tickets to an event. She wanted to be a positive influence in the family and expressed her love in tangible ways. She did not expect her DIL to reciprocate; being kind was enough for Martha.

What is helpful in mending poor relationships? Scripture. "Search me, God, and know my heart; test me and know my anxious thoughts. See if there is any offensive way in me and lead me in the way everlasting" (Psalm 139:23-24). Consider your role in the poor relationship. As much as you would like to blame others for difficult and tense relationships, praying about your own attitude of resentment can create change.

Choose to be thoughtful, kind, and forgiving. If it's not your first instinct (and we all need to work on it), ask for God's guidance. By doing so, you will help the next generation see mercy, grace, and wisdom in seniors. Keep in mind, your DIL or SIL will probably be a mother-in-law or father-in-law someday and see things in a different light. Your words and actions now will be a good model for the future.

TEN TIPS FOR SMOOTH FAMILY RELATIONSHIPS

1. Let the peacemaking begin with you.
2. Expect the best, not the worst.
3. Choose not to retaliate against perceived slights or even legitimate ones.
4. Always pray for direction and wisdom from God for improvement in relationships.
5. Speak truth without blame and be willing to risk pain. It often hurts to work things out.
6. Accept the role of grandparent.
7. Practice the Golden Rule: "Do to others as you would have them do to you" (Luke 6:31).
8. Show kindness to your adult children, their spouses, and the grandchildren.

9. If you have multiple adult children, honor the confidentiality of one family concerning another.

10. Don't be tempted to talk about family members, as gossip is never helpful.

IN SUMMARY: BANNERS FROM THE BLEACHERS

- Be creative in connecting with out-of-town grandchildren.
- Consistently pray for grandchildren who have abandoned their faith.
- Discipline is best when Grandma and Grandpa are on the same page as Mom and Dad.
- Accept the in-laws as an integral part of your family.

CHAPTER 9

Grateful Grandchildren Remember

This chapter is filled with memories that grandchildren of all ages shared about their own grandparents. We hope you enjoy reading these blessings! Thanks to all who shared their memories. Hopefully, these ideas will create a spark in you to reminisce on the various ways your own grandparents influenced you and will inspire you to connect in new and deeper ways with your own grandkids. The last page is especially for you! Record your grandparent memories to share with your grandchildren.

BECKY REMEMBERS …

The reason I could contribute to this book is because I was blessed with a grandmother who was a tremendous gift to me. She loved completely, without reservation, each one of her three grandchildren: my sister, brother, and me. I have so many stories of how she lived her life with an attitude of gratitude. One snapshot of our relationship is a story I wrote for a book about love and faith shared by the women in our lives, Mother of Pearl: Luminous Lessons and Iridescent Faith. Here's a part of the story. My grandmother, Kit Kat, and I were coconspirators from early on.

"Easter, when the earthy smell of spring hangs in the air, colorful crocus and daffodils emerge from the snow, and church bells announce the resurrection of the Risen King. Every Easter, tall white lilies encased the communion table in my family's church. The sights and sounds of childhood Easter celebrations are memories I hold in my heart.

One particular Easter Sunday long ago, I remember wiggling free from my parents and maneuvering to sit between my grandparents. With my spiffy new white patent leather shoes and matching purse, I snuggled closer to them in the pew. During the service, I stealthily took chocolate eggs from my pocketbook, peeled the foil wrappers, and popped the treats, one by one, into my mouth. My grandma would reach over, palm up, to collect the wrappers and quietly deposit them in her own purse. I was sure my mom never noticed. That was my grandma: friend, confidante, and partner in crime ... even if it was only eating chocolate in church."[16]

No one in my family recalls why we called her Kit Kat instead of Grandma, but she was Kit Kat long before Hershey's introduced the candy bar. The nickname fit her well. She was sweet, funny, and the life of the party.

Kit Kat was the one I'd often turn to for guidance and a listening ear. She had many years of life experience to advise and encourage as well as time to listen. I would talk endlessly. She would listen patiently. Afterward, Kit Kat would provide suggestions to improve a sticky situation or mend a broken friendship. Her final comment after offering wise counsel was, "I'll keep you in my prayers, Lovey." And I know she was true to her word. Her own reliance on prayer nurtured my prayer life. My first Bible was from Kit Kat and Papa, my grandfather.

---

16   Margaret McSweeney, *Mother of Pearl: Luminous Lessons and Iridescent Faith* (Bloomington: Inspiring Voices, 2012) 20.

My grandmother taught me to underline and take notes in my Bible to learn, remember, and return to when I needed encouragement. As an adult, that practice translated into studying God's Word and praying scripture. Because the 23rd Psalm was incredibly significant to her, especially when my grandfather was ill, it's important to me.

She encouraged me to be brave too. As the only child of a mother who was the eldest of eight, she was a take charge kind of gal. My mom was Kit Kat's only child and I'm my mother's eldest. (I use this lineage as an excuse for my occasional bossiness.) These strong women taught me that a capable mama is an asset to a family.

All the major and many of the minor events in my life were spent with my grandmother. She moved me into the college dorm my freshman year and attended graduation with my whole family four years later. Every week during my college years there would be a letter in my post office box with news from home and a little cash, just in case the food wasn't up to par. The weekly missive from my grandma was a connection to home and a word of encouragement from my cheerleader.

My boys loved their great grandma too. Ryan and Eric have fond memories of time spent with Kit Kat. Christmas was a very special holiday, especially Christmas Eve. The fireplace would be crackling, the tree would be laden with gifts, and the smells from the kitchen would make our mouths water. As we would walk in the front door, the kids would make a mad dash to Kit Kat's grand piano in the living room. Each year, she decorated the entire lid with a winter wonderland scene which included a mirrored ice rink with skaters, sparkling trees nestled into a snowy landscape, and a lit church on a hilltop overlooking a festive village.

I loved Kit Kat and appreciated her with all my heart. But it wasn't until I was much older that I realized how greatly she had influenced my life and how blessed my whole family was to have her as our matriarch and role model. Someday, if and when I'm a grandma, I will endeavor to live up to her example by coming alongside the next generation with love and tenderness. Kit Kat lived to be 101 years old. Her legacy of love truly lives on in my extended family. Kit Kat made the world a brighter place by sharing her joy. I pray I have her propensity for happiness, gratitude, and faith… always.

CAROL REMEMBERS …

My grandmother died two years before I was born; however, she still had a great impact on my life. All my growing up years, I heard stories about her kindness, compassion, hospitality, and desire to help others. She was known for her deep faith and love of family and her church: Our Savior's Lutheran Church. I was always told by my great aunts that I looked like her and had many of her mannerisms. This made me want to strive to be inwardly more like her. Even though I never met Grandma Aagaard, she has always been a role model for me.

ERIC REMEMBERS …

I have many vivid remembrances of my grandparents. Each of them had special significance to me. Both grandmothers showed me unconditional love and tried their hardest to fatten me up while I resisted by only wanting certain bland food. Today, I definitely regret my cuisine choices back then because they were both wonderful cooks — and now I eat and enjoy all types of foods. My two grandfathers taught me how to work hard, whether it was scraping and painting a house or working around the cabin. They always were teaching us and wanting us to be engaged in their projects.

Of all the memories I have, one stands out the most. It happened when my grandparents were staying with us because my parents were out of town. I was a senior in high school and went to a party at the pastor's house. One could say my judgment was both good and not so good. I decided to sleepover and not drive home that night, and in the morning, to just sneak back in the house before my grandparents woke up. When I made this decision, it was late, and I did not want to wake my grandparents by phoning them.

When I got home the next morning, I pulled the car into the garage. When I opened the door to the house, I looked across the kitchen and saw both of my grandparents with worried — and relieved — looks on their faces. The next thing I knew, my grandma was running as fast as she could toward me and gave me a great big hug. In all my years, I had never seen her move so fast!

One of them had gone to the bathroom in the middle of the night and, unfortunately, I had left my bedroom light on, so they knew I was still out. They had spent most of the night worried that something had happened to me, so when I popped my head through the door, they were very excited to see me. Of course, they were not happy with me, but their relief was much greater than their anger. Eventually, this experience brought us closer together and became one of the collective stories that each family has and continues to tell as it's passed down through the generations.

MAGGIE REMEMBERS ...

A friend's grandma would send cookies to college every few weeks. What a joy to be a secondary recipient of THAT package! I'm glad he always shared!

LIV REMEMBERS ...

Looking back on my childhood, I have a thousand positive memories with my grandparents. All of my grandparents have played substantial roles in so many different ways in my life. One of my favorite memories has to be when they whisked my sister and me to the Creation Museum in Kentucky when we were little girls. I'll never forget seeing tree frogs and my favorite, a platypus. My grandma and grandpa have done everything in their power to make sure my sisters and I could not only have strong faith, but experience it, too. It was amazing at such a young age to see so many Bible stories I heard on Sundays come alive.

LAURIE REMEMBERS ...

My Grandpa Howdo was a simple guy. His real name was Roy, but he got his nickname from the sock puppets he made with us. Each puppet show would start with introductions as he asked us, "How do you do?"

Grandpa had to quit school in eighth grade to help on the family farm. He was never bitter about this, but instead taught me to appreciate the gift of a good education, working hard, and how it will pay off later in life.

Sleepovers at my grandparent's house would always include a walk to the corner drugstore to get a gum ball out of the penny machine. We would stop along the way to pick snapdragons and to visit with neighbors. Grandma and Grandpa would let us stay up late to watch the Lawrence Welk Show. They would encourage my two sisters and me to sing together like the Lennon Sisters, with the hope that someday, we too, could be on the Lawrence Welk Show.

Grandpa Howdo was a gentle man who taught me the value of hard work and how to appreciate simple pleasures of life.

ERIC REMEMBERS ...

As a little kid, I loved my time at Pleasant Grove Farm with Grandma and Grandpa. Coffee Time, when we'd all come in from the wheat fields to have treats as a family, was the best. I got to have coffee with the adults. Grandma and Grandpa let my brother, Ryan, and me watch cartoons and eat strawberries with lots of sugar.

My other grandparents, Gram and Doc, would have my family to their island. We would fish, shoot clay targets, and make s'mores in the fireplace. It was so funny when Doc would feed his dog, Rusty, whipped cream.

CINDY REMEMBERS ...

When I think of the word grandparents, the first words that come to mind are love and support. I don't have many memories of my own grandparents, but my children's grandparents have supported us through the lowest of the lows and the highest of the highs, through tears of happiness and tears of sadness. I feel they have the toughest job of all because they are not only feeling for the grandchildren, but also their own children. They are strong, non-judgmental, and wise with their words. My children are blessed because their grandparents not only share their experiences openly and honestly but also their love of the Lord and our country. So, in my opinion, there is no more important role than that of a grandparent. They are our role models.

GABRIELLE REMEMBERS ...

My family was in California on vacation. My cousin and I did water aerobics in the motion pool with our grandpa. It was so much fun laughing together as we tried to keep up with the instructor. I always look forward every year to baking Christmas cookies with my grandmother and my cousin. The dough tastes so good but best of all is just hanging together.

HANNAH REMEMBERS ...

My grandmother was sure the cafeteria food would be terrible, and I would suffer during my college years. Every week she would write, filling me in on the news from home. The envelope always included a few dollars. She signed each letter with a postscript, "P.S. In case the food is bad and you're hungry, buy a cheeseburger and malt on me."

ANNE REMEMBERS ...

My grandfather was a marvelous storyteller. I have wonderful memories of Daddy Bert calling his grandchildren to gather around him for a story after dinner. He had an imaginary "sprite" who sat on his shoulder and whispered the story in Daddy Bert's ear. He would announce, "The Sprite has a new story to share." He would act as if he was hearing the story from the Sprite, turn his head to his left shoulder, and even ask the Sprite a question or two. Then, a wondrous story would unfold. I felt surrounded by love and wonder with my parents, grandparents, cousins, aunts, and uncles gathered all together. Thanks Becky and Carol for stirring this delightful memory!

MIKE REMEMBERS ...

My Grandpa Louis bought a brand-new Chevy pickup in 1986. My Dad and I drove up for Thanksgiving and then we went to Grand Forks about 30 miles away in the new truck. Dad drove there, but

Grandpa said I could drive back. I was so excited, yet a little nervous, as I only had my permit and had never driven a "new" truck. It is amazing to remember. My brother Pat still has that truck so every time I see it, I think of that day and Grandpa.

JILLIAN REMEMBERS …

I am in a unique position as the oldest grandchild in my family. Having known my grandparents for 22 years, I have been able to experience their energy and imagination as we played with my toddler toys, their knowledge and patience as they taught me about sewing, baking, and golf, and their unconditional love for and deep appreciation of always-too-short time with family.

While my younger cousins had similar experiences, there is something to be said about knowing my grandparents in *their* younger years. I got to know them for who they truly are, before the challenges of age began to place limits on what they were able to do. I am also able to fully comprehend the important role they have played in my life and attempt to thank them enough for all they have done.

My grandparents were there when I was trying to take my first steps, holding my hand and cheering me on. Now, I am able to return the favor by carrying their bags, helping them into the car, and jogging their memory when things just seem to slip away.

Thanks to the stories shared by my grandparents, I have learned that family is much more than each individual member. Knowing and understanding where I come from and what shaped those that came before me is critical to establishing a true sense of self. I am forever grateful to have learned from my grandparents and excited to pass along the lessons that they have instilled in me.

GREG REMEMBERS ...

There is nothing more special for a child than to have a solid relationship with grandparents. Mine were special in different ways, but they all taught me about living a good life. My family and I are blessed to have taken over my grandparents' cabin. The smell, the artwork, and even the squeak of the fireplace reminds me of them. I still fish at Grandpa's secret "hot spots" and pick blueberries in Grandma's hidden berry patch with my children.

My other grandfather collected quotes, and after he died, the family put them all in a book for the family. The quotes about life are powerful, and when needed, I can still turn to his wisdom and faith through that book of quotes. Both grandmothers had kind and gentle souls. I have great memories of our times together.

KIKI REMEMBERS ...

Grandparents are important to me because they are like super-heroes. Whenever we need help or just want to be with them, they will come be with us! They help us to be better people and help us to grow as better students, children, and siblings! Grandparents are giving and caring to us. They bring us places and always make sure we are happy! They spoil us big time! But even without being spoiled, we love them and always look forward to spending time with them!

ANN REMEMBERS ...

My grandparents gave me my first Bible when I was 10 years old. *The Children's Bible*, with beautifully illustrated pictures, is still a treasure.

SCOTT REMEMBERS ...

Grandpa Stan was a "tool guy." He and I would spend time in his basement working on little projects. We would work on his miniature steam engine, too, which was really fun. He was a great role model in trusting in God. When difficulties arose, he would often say, "Do not charge your soul with care. Give the problem to God." His wise words have stuck with me through the years.

CINDY REMEMBERS ...

My Grandma Mabel was a very important person in my life and spending time with her at her house was one of my favorite things. I loved sleeping over at her house, even as a teenager. She always had wonderful treats including her famous "Grandma Rolls."

She was a great listener. I could share things with her that I couldn't with my mom, and I knew she would give me the best advice. I still think of her often and am so grateful for the relationship that we had. Although she had dementia the last few years of her life, she was able to meet and hold each of my children in her arms.

RYAN REMEMBERS ...

One of my favorite memories with Gram and Doc is when we were walleye fishing up at Spider Island, right before a storm. The walleyes were biting like crazy, and together we caught quite a few fish. Doc had taught me all of the tricks and tips to get the most bites. After heading back to the island before the storm rolled in, Gram masterfully cooked the fresh walleye, and we all enjoyed a delicious meal together. To cap off the night, we sat on the porch together eating homemade popcorn and enjoying an incredible light show playing over the lake in the distance.

My favorite memories of times with Grandma Shirley and Grandpa Rollie, my dad's parents, was time spent up at the family farm. It was fun to learn from Grandpa Rollie how all of the different tractors and implements worked, and how to use them. I remember sitting next to him in the buddy seat on the tractor as we plowed and seeded the fields. Grandma Shirley had an incredible garden at the farm, and I have many fond memories of helping her plant different flowers.

MOLLIE REMEMBERS ...

I had each grandchild draw/paint a self-portrait for Grandma and Grandpa. The portraits were then framed. They still hang, to this day, at Grandma's and Grandpa's home and always bring a smile.

JOAN REMEMBERS ...

I have the sweetest memory of my maternal grandmother. A kind and gentle woman, she married young and knew the demanding work of living on a farm in rural Wisconsin, supporting animal care and field work, but she also tackled daily household challenges: washing clothes, feeding a large family, putting up canned fruits and vegetables, chopping wood, and so much more. In spite of the many demands on her time, she was an excellent baker. Some of my earliest memories are of walking into her kitchen (the warmth of the oven outdone only by the warmth of her selfless love) as she was taking hot, fresh loaves of homemade bread, all brown and crusty and fragrant, out of the oven. She helped us cut into it while it was far too warm, and we happily slathered creamy butter on top (with no thought of cholesterol clogging or saturated fats). And she looked on lovingly, as we ate our fill. Even today, the memory warms my soul.

RACHAEL REMEMBERS ...

I am going to share ten lessons I learned from my grandma, some because she reminded me over and over, and some by how she lived her life.

1. She taught me how to make fruit cake, jam cookies, and other family favorites.
2. She taught me in the kitchen to always clean up as you go along. I didn't fully appreciate this until I lived in my own tiny kitchen.
3. Always have one or two songs that you can play from memory on the piano.
4. Always put your napkin in your lap and keep your elbows off the table because some day you might be invited to have dinner at the White House.
5. Be practical, especially about what you have in your kitchen and in your closets.
6. Write thank you notes.
7. Be thankful for our great country and those who preserved our freedom.
8. Ask good questions. Take interest in the interests of those you love. Stay curious.
9. Find joy in not only in the blessings God has given you, but in the blessings He has given to others.
10. Delight in God's Word and treasure it.

LILLIAN REMEMBERS ...

My favorite memories of my grandparents are from the summers I spent with them at the cabin. Specifically, the times when it was just the three of us. I look back on the Bible studies, mealtimes, and even the odd jobs around the house I was asked to do. I was lucky to learn so many lessons, even if I wasn't always happy to be learning them as a disgruntled teenager. I gained some awareness of what it means to be an upstanding Christian, a polite young woman, and selfless servant for others during those times. Sitting around the table and passing stories back and forth was the best of times.

KITTY REMEMBERS ...

My dear Grami lived to be 106 and was sharp until the end! We studied God's Word together at BSF (Bible Study Fellowship) for many years and always enjoyed singing hymns of praise to our heavenly Father at her retirement home chapel services. I would hold her hand and try to memorize the sound and feel of her warmth and presence each time. She deeply loved my Grandpa, and they always held hands. Her marriage advice for me was to "always hold hands," which I have loved doing with my sweetheart of 34 years.

She was raised in the roaring '20s and was known for her excellent ballroom dancing skills. Her "dance card" was always full. When we were young, her hands led each of us grandkids around the living room, trying to "pass on" her skills to us. Once, as a Centenarian, she was interviewed by a TV crew who asked, "How do you stay so young looking and strong?" She jumped up and easily demonstrated her secret of staying young at heart, by showing her dance moves in her tiny kitchen. We all smiled and cheered her on, as she encouraged us to always dance. I experience peace and joy knowing Jesus took her hand, and she's now dancing in heaven.

REBECCA REMEMBERS ...

Grandma was great at knitting and crocheting. She made slippers, doll clothes, and Christmas ornaments for the tree.

What is your favorite memory of your grandparents?

Conclusion

We are to be a light to the world (Matthew 5:14), shining the light of Jesus on everyone we encounter, starting with our children and grandchildren. This command doesn't end at a specific age but continues throughout life. "They will still bear fruit in old age, they will stay fresh and green ..." (Psalm 92:14). You *can* make a positive difference in the life of your grandchildren. You *can* teach, inspire, encourage, and guide. We encourage you to stay *fresh and green* in speaking truth into the lives of your grandchildren.

Never take for granted the blessings of your family, and especially, your grandchildren. They may not be perfect, or follow in exactly the path you had hoped, but they are God's gift (Psalm 127:3 NLT). Let them know you care with unconditional love.

As a grandparent, wave your banners with enthusiasm! Encourage your grandkids to be the young men and women God has created each one to be, for the Lord. Love with your whole heart. The relationships you make with your grandchildren will not only benefit them but set the stage for future generations. May your influence be a gift that keeps on giving!

Acknowledgements

Thank you to all who reminisced on the gifts of love and faith your grandparents provided through the years. The profound impact of a grandparent's influence is carried on in the lives of the children they love and lift up in prayer. I'm incredibly grateful for my grandmother, Kit Kat, who loved my siblings and me fully and extravagantly. Her legacy is carried on through my own mom, Carole, in how she loves her grandchildren.

Thank you to all the grandchildren who shared their grandparents' faith-filled and loving gestures. We couldn't have done it without you! — *Becky*

As the grandmother of eight, I can only say I wish I had gathered this information before my first grandchild was born. I would have better understood my role and taken greater advantage of the many opportunities for building relationships. There are times I thought I hit a homerun, only to discover it was a ground ball or strike out.

My husband and I are very fortunate; our grandchildren have added an amazing joy to our lives. Each one is a special gift from God. In true "Lake Wobegon" style, our grandchildren are all above average. They are amazing, each one with his or her own abilities, gifts and personality. The day brightens whenever one of the grandchildren reaches out to us via text message or phone call or when a grandchild asks to spend time with us. They are a link into this new generation. They are a blessing!

A warm thank you to the many friends who shared their ideas and strategies for successful grandparenting. I appreciate their thoughts, impressions, disappointments, humor, and advice. — *Carol*

Notes

CHAPTER 2 NOTES

1. Tom Moe, "*Some Rules for a Young Athlete.*" Used with permission of the author.

CHAPTER 4 NOTES

2. Harvard Medical School, https://www.health.harvard.edu/healthbeat/giving-thanks-can-make-you-happier. Accessed 02-33-21.

CHAPTER 5 NOTES

3. American College of Pediatricians, https://www.acpeds.org/the-college-speaks/position-statements/parenting-issues/the-benefits-of-the-family-table Accessed 02-23-21.

4. Copyright © 2011 by the American Academy of Pediatrics, https://pediatrics.aappublications.org/content/127/6/e1565.full Accessed 02-23-21.

CHAPTER 6 NOTES

5. Ron Blue, *Splitting Heirs: Giving Your Money and Things to Your Children Without Ruining Their Lives,* Northfield Publishing: Chicago. 2004 p. 76.

6. ibid. p. 91.

CHAPTER 7 NOTES

7.   Mulvihill, Dr. Josh, RenewaNation: Helping Children Develop a Biblical Worldview. https://www.renewanation.org/post/understanding-the-biblical-role-of-grandparents. Accessed 02-23-21.

8.   Dr. Kara E. Powell and Dr. Chap Clark, *Sticky Faith: Everyday Ideas to Build Lasting Faith in Your Kids* (Grand Rapids: Zondervan, 2011), 23.

9.   Pew Research Center on Social Demographic Trend, December 17, 2015. "Parenting in America," https://www.pewresearch.org/social-trends/2015/12/17/1-the-american-family-today/. Accessed 02-23-21.

10.   ibid.

11.   Beliefnet.com, https://www.beliefnet.com/prayables/galleries/funniest-grandparent-jokes.aspx?p=7. Accessed 02-03-20.

12.   Walsh, Dr. David, Spark and Stitch Institute. https://sparkandstitchinstitute.com/media-influence-whoever-tells-the-stories-defines-the-culture/. Accessed 02-03-20.

13.   ibid.

CHAPTER 8 NOTES

14.   https://albertmohler.com/2016/01/20/the-scandal-of-biblical-illiteracy-its-our-problem-4/. Accessed 02/23/21.

15.   Karl Pillemer, Ph.D., *Fault Line: Fractured Families and How to Mend Them* (New York: Penguin Random House, 2020), 244.

CHAPTER 9 NOTES

16.   Margaret McSweeney, *Mother of Pearl: Luminous Lessons and Iridescent Faith* (Bloomington: Inspiring Voices, 2012), 20.

About the Authors

BECKY DANIELSON, M.ED.

Becky's favorite title is *Mom*. She and her husband, Scott, have two adult sons and live in the Twin Cities with their golden retriever puppy. She is a former elementary school teacher with a BA in Elementary Education, an MA in Education, and licensure in Early Childhood Education and Parent and Family Education. Following Jesus and sharing God's Word to equip and encourage families is Becky's life work. She works with parents privately, in small and large groups, and at a Christian preschool working with both parents and staff. Becky candidly shares her life as a Christian wife, mom, and educator in small group settings and at national conferences. She is the co-author of *Raising Little Kids with Big Love, Raising Big Kids with Supernatural Love,* both with study guides, and *Empowered Parents: Putting Faith First.* She blogs for moms and dads at FaithFirstParent.com.

CAROL OLSEN

 Since graduating from Iowa State University, Carol has spent more than 40 years in the field of education. She taught high school home economics, co-authored the craft book *Brass and Beads*, and co-directed, as well as hosted, the cable television program *Mrs. Olsen's Neighborhood*. As a licensed parent educator, Carol developed and provided oversight for the Edina Family Resource Center, a part of the school district's community education. Over the past 18 years, Carol has taught and lectured both children and adults on America's Christian heritage and Christian worldview. In 2013, she authored the family book *America's Forgotten Heritage* after realizing how little her grandchildren knew about the part Christianity played in the founding of the United States. As an Elder of Christ Presbyterian Church in Edina, she worked primarily in children's ministry and in 2005 developed a vacation Bible school curriculum centered on Christian heritage. Carol and her husband Neil have been married for 56 active years. They have three married children and eight grandchildren.

Additional Titles

America's Forgotten Heritage
by Carol Olsen

Raising Little Kids with Big Love
Raising Little Kids with Big Love Study Guide
Raising Big Kids with Supernatural Love
Raising Big Kids with Supernatural Love Study Guide
Empowered Parents: Putting Faith First
by Becky Danielson and Lori Wildenberg